DANGER
CALLING

DANGER
CALLING
TRUE ADVENTURES OF RISK AND FAITH

PEB JACKSON
JAMES LUND

Revell
a division of Baker Publishing Group
Grand Rapids, Michigan

© 2010 by James L. Lund

Published by Revell
a division of Baker Publishing Group
P.O. Box 6287, Grand Rapids, MI 49516-6287
www.revellbooks.com

Printed in the United States of America

Library of Congress Cataloging-in-Publication Data
Jackson, Peb.
    Danger calling : true adventures of risk and faith / Peb Jackson, James Lund.
        p.   cm.
    Includes bibliographical references.
    ISBN 978-0-8007-3404-6 (pbk.)
    1. Christian life. 2. Risk taking (Psychology)—Religious aspects—Christianity. 3. Adventure and adventurers. I. Lund, James L. II. Title.
    BV4598.15.J33 2010
    248.4—dc22   2010013620

Published in association with William K. Jensen Literary Agency, 119 Bampton Court, Eugene, Oregon 97404.

10   11   12   13   14   15   16   7   6   5   4   3   2   1

To my longtime friend Tim Hansel and the gang at Summit Expedition, who fired me up in countless ways, especially in reference to mountains and great effort.

Peb

To Betty Jean (Leonard) Lund, who encouraged me to pursue my calling wherever it led. Thanks, Mom, for everything.

Jim

Contents

Acknowledgments

Most of my pursuits of adventure and opportunities in the wild were inspired by friends and by books. I vividly recall leafing through a coffee table book, *The Earth and Great Weather*. I found a picture of a canyon with steep walls above the Arctic Circle that mesmerized me—a dramatic vista indeed. I said, "I am going there someday." Ten years later, I was tromping through that exact canyon in the Brooks Range in Alaska. All of my expectations were exceeded. That scenario has been repeated many times over the past decades and I am sure will be duplicated in years to come.

A bookmark that my friend Scott McOwen and I had made for Guttenberg's, a bookstore we built, had as its tagline, "A man can't have too many books or too many friends." I have been powerfully motivated, inspired, and blessed by an abundance of both.

I want to acknowledge my partner in this venture, Jim Lund, and the indefatigable nature of this guy's disciplined conscientiousness in his writing. What a gift he has been to me in the re-creation and telling of these marvelous stories. Thank you, Jim.

To my wife, Sharon, who still flinches when I talk about ice climbing or any such pursuits, but at least has not attached a tether to my ankle . . . yet. But in reality she is my consistent, joyful partner, adventuring through this life.

Peb

Some people are called not only to dangerous adventures in life and faith but also to generously share their time, stories, and insights with pesky writers. This book would not have been possible without the help and patience of, among others, Eric Alexander, B. J. Kramps, Leon Lamprecht, Melissa Neugebauer, Todd Pierce, Dick Savidge, Drew Wills, Jeanie Wills, and my partner in publishing, the incomparable Peb Jackson. My deep thanks to each of you.

Thanks also go to our agent, Bill Jensen, the man with a million great ideas; to our editor, Andrea Doering, who patiently steered us home; and to everyone at Baker Publishing Group who played a part in enabling us to present these stories.

To Jon Coulter and the Sisters Young Life study group, thanks for the "test run." To Gil McCormick for your insights and encouragement and to Jodi Carroll for all that you do. I appreciate it.

A special word of gratitude goes to Tom Stoerzbach for invaluable research and writing assistance. Tom, you saved the day.

Last and certainly not least, I thank my family for their encouragement and support: my wife, Angela; my children, Erik, Sonja, and Peter; and my brother, Dave, who also contributed research and writing help. You guys are the best.

Jim

Introduction

This isn't your typical Bible study. We're going to take you on a high-adrenaline ride to places few people dare to venture—the rarified air at the peak of Mount Everest, the black waters at the bottom of the Atlantic, the steaming jungles of the Philippines, and the frozen floes of the Antarctic. We'll also take you to a few other places just as dangerous and thrilling—the depths of your heart, life, and faith.

You don't need a theology degree for *Danger Calling*. This is a book of true stories. It features people in extreme circumstances, often brought on by their own extreme choices. Some stories will be familiar. Some have never been told before. All will keep you in suspense, with lives hanging on every decision.

This is also a book of questions. We're going to challenge you to think about your response to each story and what it means to you. You'll find no pat answers. We'll explore four primary themes—sacrifice, perseverance, courage, and leadership—with questions such as these: *Would you stop to help a climber in the Death Zone on Everest? How much are you willing to risk for fame and glory? What is your source of strength in a crisis? Could you lead men and women into battle knowing some are likely to die?*

Part of our goal is to help you discover who you are. But we also want you to find out who you were meant to be. We want you to know where you stand in your faith. Through this book, we're asking: *Do you have a relationship with God? Are you a little too comfortable in your faith? Is he calling you to a life of greater risk and deeper meaning?*

We are a couple of guys who are fascinated by the often-hidden benefits of risk and danger and how they connect to faith. Peb is the true adventurer. As a youth, he scaled the ten-story water tower in his hometown of Haviland, Kansas (unroped). He's been testing his limits on mountains, bike trails, rapids, and jungle safaris ever since. Jim is the writer who can't decide which he loves more—a great hike in the wilderness or a great story about one. We had a good time joining forces on our first book of adventure stories, *A Dangerous Faith*. We wanted to go further, to reach into the hearts of men and women and lead them to their calling. Inspired by conversations with our agent, Bill Jensen, we began talking about a new project that would challenge readers with provocative questions about life and faith. We desire to invite today's men and women into an adventure that's as old as our existence: "Seek me and live" (Amos 5:4). The result is in your hands.

How you approach *Danger Calling* is up to you. The sixteen stories and accompanying questions are designed for talking over in a small group, but you can certainly tackle them in a larger group, with just one friend, or on your own. The idea is to read one story before you meet with your group and then go through the follow-up material for that story. *Would You? Could You?* features probing questions and relevant Scripture passages. Use it to think about what you want to say to the group. As you go through it, write down other verses to share and discuss. *Reporting In* is your invitation to connect with the Lord through prayer, either as a group or individually. *Hitting the Trail* is a section just for you, an opportunity to write down and apply whatever you're learning.

New Territory lists more questions and books, videos, and other resources to explore when you want to dig deeper.

When you meet with your group, be honest and open about your ideas and doubts. You won't get much out of this book if you say only what others want to hear. Remember to give everyone a chance to share, and encourage each other to tell your own stories of danger and faith. Allow time to thoroughly discuss each question. Depending on the dynamics of your group, feel free to take on more stories in a session. And once you're done with *Danger Calling*, don't just throw it away. Wait a few months or a year, then go through it again. You may be surprised by how much your life and faith have changed.

You won't always be comfortable with the questions in this book—or your answers. That's okay. You're starting a daring adventure, and risk and adventure are never easy. The Lord designed it that way. He uses our struggles and our proximity to danger to draw us closer to him. We find him on that precarious ridge between the comfortable and the unknown. It's where we need to be. It's the place where we discover that the more we risk and trust God, the closer we move to his heart and the higher calling for which he created us.

Thank you for joining us on this journey. Are you ready? It's time to dive deeper into danger and nearer to the Author of the greatest adventure of all.

PART ONE

SACRIFICE

1

Death Zone

When he saw him, he took pity on him.
Luke 10:33

You're alone at twenty-seven thousand feet on what the native Sherpas call *Chomolungma*, or "goddess mother of the world." It's Everest to everyone else, the world's highest and most famous mountain. The temperature is minus twenty degrees Fahrenheit. Icicles cling to your beard, your hands tingle ominously, and you can no longer feel your toes inside your climbing boots. You're exhausted, and at this altitude, five miles above sea level, it takes at least four deep breaths to gather enough energy for a single step. Somewhere in the recesses of your mind, a warning siren sounds. You know Everest is deadly. More than two hundred people have died here since Sir Edmund Hillary and Tenzing Norgay first scaled the summit in 1953.

But you're not thinking about the danger. You're caught up in the dream. You've been climbing since age eleven when you first watched a TV documentary about Hillary. You love the thrill of focusing every aspect of mind and body on that next precarious step, that next tantalizing handhold. It's what makes you feel alive. You've devoted thousands of hours, and dollars, to this sport. You've climbed Elbrus in Russia, Denali in Alaska, Aconcagua in Argentina. It seems as if your entire life has been preparation for this day, this moment.

I'm almost there, you think. *Just another two thousand feet.*

Step.

Breathe.

Almost there.

Britain's David Sharp is another climber who badly wants to reach the summit of Everest. The thirty-four-year-old engineer has already come close twice, once as part of an expedition and once on a solo attempt. Both times, a combination of weather conditions, frostbite, and lack of oxygen forced him to turn back. He lost parts of two toes in the process.

But in May 2006, he is back on Everest for what he sees as his final try at the roof of the world. He has better gear this time, including a pair of red Millet Everest knee boots, and is determined to succeed. He tells a fellow climber, "I would give up more toes, or even fingers, to get on top."

On this trip, Sharp is loosely affiliated with an expedition outfit called Asian Trekking International, but he is essentially climbing alone, as he'd planned. Before leaving for Nepal, he told his mother in England, "You are never on your own. There are climbers everywhere."

In the first week of May, from base camp at 17,060 feet, Sharp launches his bid for the summit. He reaches the North Col and establishes a camp at about 25,920 feet, but snow and wind on the third day force him to retreat.

While at advance base camp, he discusses the use of bottled oxygen with a climbing guide. The guide is a purist who advocates climbing by "fair means," though only a small percentage of the climbers who successfully summit Everest do so without oxygen. Sharp tells the guide he plans to use gas only in an extreme emergency. As far as the guide can tell, Sharp has but one four-liter cylinder.

The oxygen issue is not an idle one. The threat of "mountain sickness"—including the deadly pulmonary or cerebral edema—hangs over every high-altitude climber. In the case of pulmonary edema, the combination of low oxygen pressure and high exertion can force fluid into the millions of small, elastic air sacs inside a person's lungs. If the fluid builds up enough so the air sacs can no longer absorb oxygen, the victim essentially drowns on the inside. With cerebral edema, it is the brain that swells with fluid, creating pressure inside the skull. Some people are more susceptible than others, and the precise cause is still a mystery.

Of course, any of the symptoms of severe mountain sickness—extreme shortness of breath, fatigue, coughing, blood in the sputum, stumbling, lack of coordination, hearing or seeing things, drowsiness—can be fatal to a climber laboring in harsh conditions on a Himalayan mountain. The use of bottled oxygen can at least delay the effects of these symptoms.

On May 11, presumably with his lone oxygen bottle, David Sharp resumes his quest to reach the pinnacle of Everest. Three days later, a little after 1 a.m., Colorado guide Bill Crouse and several fellow climbers encounter Sharp in the darkness at approximately 27,560 feet. Sharp sits down and unclips from the fixed rope to let the group pass. The climbers wave gloved hands at each other. No one has time or energy for conversation.

More than ten hours later, a little after 11 a.m., Crouse and his team have already summitted and descended to the top of a rock band known as the Third Step, just 490 vertical feet below Everest's peak. They are trying to move quickly, before their oxygen runs out and in hopes of avoiding a bottleneck of climbers farther down. The group again sees Sharp, now at the base of the Third Step. He's clipped to the fixed line but is off to the side, out of the wind. Crouse and his team continue to descend, unclipping from the line to move around Sharp.

"Watch out," Crouse tells Sharp as he passes. There is no reply.

About an hour and twenty minutes later, Crouse looks back and sees Sharp has moved up another three hundred feet. It appears no one else is ascending. "That guy's heading up pretty late," he says to another climber. About 2 p.m., Crouse glances up the route and spies Sharp one last time. He's past the Third Step, but he has advanced only another hundred yards toward the summit.

David Sharp's activities for the next several hours are lost to history.

Early the next morning, just before 1 a.m., an ascending film team reaches an alcove at the base of the technical pitch called the First Step. They are at 27,760 feet. The team's guide expects to find a body there, the victim of a disastrous 1996 storm and who is now known to climbers as "Green Boots." But the guide is startled when his headlamp illuminates a second body tucked beneath the overhang. This figure's boots are red.

A closer examination reveals a climber still clipped to the red-and-blue guide rope, sitting with his arms wrapped around his knees. He is alive but has no oxygen mask on. Ice crystals have formed on his closed eyelashes. His nose is black. The guide yells at the man to get moving, but there is no response. Believing the man is in a hypothermic coma and sadly beyond help, the guide decides to move on. "Rest in peace," a climber says as he leaves.

About twenty minutes later, an ascending Turkish group discovers "Red Boots"—Sharp—but now he is apparently

20

recovered enough to wave them off. The Turks also continue their climb.

In all, more than thirty climbers pass by the First Step overhang that morning on their way toward the summit. After the Turks, apparently, each of these climbers either does not notice the figure sitting there, or assumes it is Green Boots, or decides that there are now two dead bodies at the First Step. For the next seven hours—the critical time when, perhaps, David Sharp's life hangs in the balance—no one stops to investigate.

Finally, at about 8:30 a.m. on May 15, two Sherpas assisting their female client down the mountain discover Sharp.

"This look like new body, man," Dawa Sherpa says.

"No, this one die long time ago," the other Sherpa replies.

"No, no, he is another body, a new body."

Dawa looks closer and finds Sharp alive, but barely. His legs are frozen. His face is black. Icicles hang from his nose. Dawa unzips Sharp's down jacket to touch his chest—icy cold.

There is little the distressed Sherpas can do. Their client, who was attempting to become the first Turkish woman on the summit, collapsed and lost consciousness just eight hundred feet short of the goal and is still unstable. Both Sherpas are already exhausted, and Dawa tore muscles in his chest during a coughing fit. It will take all their strength to guide their impaired client down to safety. Reluctantly, they turn and leave.

Over the next few hours, more climbers discover Sharp and try to render aid. One group tries to pour hot water down his throat. Another administers oxygen, drags Sharp into a patch of sunlight, and tries unsuccessfully to get him to stand. Sharp revives enough to say to one Sherpa, "My name is David Sharp. I'm with Asian Trekking, and I just want to sleep."

Maxime Chaya, who earlier that day became the first Lebanese citizen to scale Everest, hadn't noticed the man with red boots on his ascent. On the way down, however, he sees Sharp and attempts to revive him. Finally realizing it is too late, Chaya sits with Sharp and weeps. Nearly an hour later, his own oxygen running out, Chaya stands, recites the Lord's Prayer, and walks away.

The next day, another Sherpa reaches the First Step. He radios that the man in the red boots is dead.

It's likely no one will ever know if David Sharp realized his dream and conquered the summit of Everest. He left no physical evidence there. His camera has disappeared. What is known is that Sharp is one of the latest, though most certainly not the last, victims of *Chomolungma*. His body will serve as a memorial to his determined and adventurous spirit—and to the risks for anyone who dares to reach for the sky.

Would You? Could You?

(Share your answers if you're reading in a group)

As vacation destinations go, the "Death Zone" on Everest will never rank very high—it's just about the most inhospitable place on the planet. Yet the more daring (some would say *crazy*) among us keep going there, and dying there. So what exactly is our obligation to our fellow man when we're standing in the middle of the jet stream? Do the rules of common human decency get suspended above, say, twenty-five thousand feet? Should anyone expect help in a place where one's own survival consumes every ounce of brain matter?

After David Sharp's demise, Max Chaya remembered, "When it was clear what state David was in—that he was much closer to death than to life—Russ [expedition leader Russell Brice, via radio] just told me, 'Max, we can't do anything. You have to come back down' . . . Russell had an obligation toward me because I'm his client. And he didn't want anyone else to jeopardize their life to try and save someone who's almost dead . . . I couldn't understand how I could walk past a dying person while being myself in 100 percent mental and physical condition, without being able to help. But I understand now."

Soon after the incident, critics from all points on the compass lined up to admonish the climbers who failed to attempt a rescue. Among them was Sir Edmund Hillary, who said that "Human life is far more important than just getting to the top of a mountain." Sharp's mother, on the other hand, didn't blame anyone for her son's death. She was quoted as saying, "Your only responsibility is to save yourself, not to try to save someone else."

Talk is cheap. The question is: What would *you* do?

- If you were at twenty-seven thousand feet on Everest, fatigued and low on oxygen, *would you* stop to help a climber in distress?
- Some clients pay as much as $65,000 for guides to lead them to Everest's peak. If your life's dream was to reach the top of the world—and if you'd emptied your bank account to make it happen—*could you* give up your dream for someone you didn't know? Does your responsibility change if the person in trouble intentionally put himself at risk?
- Read the parable of the Good Samaritan in Luke 10:25–37. Jews and Samaritans were openly hostile toward each other at this time. Given those circumstances, how much risk did the Samaritan assume by stopping?
- Jesus said that the second of the two greatest commandments is "Love your neighbor as yourself" (Matt. 22:39). How great is your love for your "neighbor"? *Would you* honestly risk your life for him or her? What if it's 90 percent likely that you'll die in the attempt? Seventy-five percent likely? Fifty-fifty? Should your answer depend on whether you are single versus married with children at home?

- When Jesus says at the end of the parable of the Good Samaritan, "Go and do likewise," does he mean that we should *always* stop to help someone in need? Jesus gave his life for us on the cross, yet during his ministry, when crowds gathered to experience his teaching and healing, he often withdrew to pray (Luke 5:15–16). Does this mean there are times when it's appropriate *not* to help others?

- When has someone taken a personal risk—physical or otherwise—to help you during a crisis? How did you feel about that person's actions? Have you ever been ready to or actually have put your life at risk for someone else? How did that make you feel about yourself?

- It takes a truckload of ambition to reach the top of Everest. How ambitious are you? In what areas of your life are you ambitious? When is ambition healthy and when is it not? Are you happy with the level of your ambition, or do you feel the need to ramp up or cut back? Why?

Reporting In

Are you struggling with any of these issues? It's time to pray for guidance. Has God given you clear direction? It's still time to pray!

Hitting the Trail

(This is just for you)

Most of us won't be hiking up Everest anytime soon, so we probably won't have to deal with a dying climber. Yet we know any number of people who are in distress. In some cases it's obvious; in others, they try to hide it. Either way, for them, the crisis is real. So . . . what are you going to do about it?

- Make a list of people you know who might be in distress. They could be co-workers, neighbors, your children, or your wife. What are their issues? What do they need? What is your plan to do something about it? Write it down here.

_____

_____

_____

- What situations are most likely to draw you in as a Good Samaritan? When are you least likely to step in? How is your reluctance in that area affecting your marriage or your relationships with others? What could you do to change that? Record it here.

_____

_____

_____

- How often do you, like David Sharp, set out to take on an enormous obstacle on your own? Is this a strength or a flaw? If you're not sure—or if you're concerned about your answer—corner a buddy and talk it over.

_____

_____

_____

New Territory

(For those who want to explore further)

Read *Into Thin Air* by Jon Krakauer, the bestselling account of the 1996 Everest tragedy. Watch season one of the Discovery Channel series *Everest: Beyond the Limit*, which was filmed at the same time as David Sharp's summit attempt and death on the mountain.

- Who are the "priests" and "Levites" and who are the "Good Samaritans" in these accounts? Do some people fall into both categories?
- How would you now judge the actions—or inactions—of the climbers on Everest during David Sharp's demise? How about David Sharp himself?

2

With Gladness

Serve the LORD with gladness;
Come before His presence with singing.

Psalm 100:2 NKJV

Only three exhausted, starving hostages are left, hiking through the soggy jungle with their captors. Over the past year, the rest of the twenty-four Filipino and American hostages have either been released for ransom payments, abandoned after being wounded in one of the frequent gun battles with government troops, or beheaded.

It's June 7, 2002, on Mindanao in the Philippines, a large island of volcanic mountains and swampy lowland plateaus that is home to most of the country's Muslims. One year and eleven days ago, armed members of a militant Islamic separatist group called Abu Sayyaf kidnapped tourists from their beds at a nearby beach resort to extort money for their radical cause.

Martin and Gracia Burnham had been celebrating their eighteenth wedding anniversary at that resort, a rare vacation indulgence given their modest income running an aviation service for the New Tribes Mission in Mindanao. Since the mid-1980s, Martin has flown in food and medicine to the natives and missionaries and has transported tribal patients to medical facilities.

When he was flying his missions, there had always been risk, and Gracia had been his ground crew, staying in constant communication by radio. But today, on this rainy afternoon in the jungle, they are side by side, physically spent by the most dangerous ordeal of their lives. Martin is a bearded skeleton compared to the handsome, fun-loving pilot who swept Gracia off her feet two decades ago.

"I just don't think I can keep doing this much longer," Gracia tells him.

"You know, Gracia, I just think we're going to get out of here soon," Martin says. "I think this is all going to work out. After we're home, this is going to seem like such a short time to us. Let's just hold steady."

The words are typical of Martin. He is always ready with more encouragement, always quick to shore up Gracia's flagging spirit.

When Sabaya, an Abu Sayyaf leader who speaks English, gives the order to make camp on the steep downslope of a mountain, Martin and Gracia huddle together in a hammock in the jungle under a makeshift cloth shelter. They do their best to comfort one another, but both know in their hearts that they may die here—that "going home" may mean going to be with their Lord.

On the run from the AFP (Armed Forces of the Philippines), hostages and captors alike are weak today, and they've been lax about covering their tracks. They had to abandon their single cooking pot during a gun battle and have eaten nothing but raw rice and some leaves from the low vegetation for the past nine days. When Sabaya caught some of his men greedily eating more than their fair share of the limited supply, he took all the rice and gave it to Martin to carry. The extra weight made the pack cut deeper into his shoulders.

"He's the only one I can trust who won't eat it," Sabaya had said to Gracia.

Martin didn't complain. He was often made to carry extra supplies, which sometimes made him slip and fall in the mud, but he never complained. When the Abu Sayyaf's satellite phone broke, he repaired it for them. As he served them, he talked to his captors and fellow hostages about his faith in Jesus, and they listened.

Today, as always when they stop to rest, Martin has made sure the other remaining hostage, a Filipino nurse who also had been abducted from the resort, has her hammock secured between sturdy trees. The nurse is settled just a short distance up the hill from Martin and Gracia as they quietly recite memorized Scriptures to one another and sing favorite hymns together in their hammock.

"I really don't know why this has happened to us," Martin says. "I've been thinking a lot lately about Psalm 100—what it says about serving the Lord with gladness. This may not seem much like serving the Lord, but that's what we're doing, you know? We may not leave this jungle alive, but we can leave this world serving the Lord with gladness. We can come before his presence with singing."

Martin and Gracia pray together for their three children back home, thank the Lord for being with them in the midst of all this, and try to take a nap.

Suddenly a stream of gunfire erupts from the top of the hill, very close to their location.

"Oh, God!" Gracia says. She's not swearing. She's praying.

She knows she needs to drop to the ground. As she swings her feet over the side of the hammock, she's aware of a bullet zinging through her right leg. She rolls eight feet down the slope and sees Martin on the ground, twisted into an unnatural position, eyes closed.

It's 1981, back at Calvary Bible College in Kansas City, where Martin and Gracia have known each other as friends for a few years. But Martin catches her off guard when he asks her for a date to the fall concert.

"Can I let you know?" she stammers.

No, you can't. Never mind then. That, he says later, was his rehearsed answer to this dreaded female evasive maneuver.

But what comes out of his mouth is, "Yeah. You can let me know."

He surprises himself with his own response, figures this gal must be something pretty special, then turns and heads for class.

She immediately checks with her girlfriends, who are enthusiastic because everybody agrees Martin is a terrific guy. She accepts.

He shows up wearing a suit she's never seen him in before, but the same cowboy boots he always wears with his flannel shirt and jeans. His dashing moustache matches his reddish hair, and his eyes twinkle at his good fortune to be with this pretty girl tonight. After the concert he takes her flying to see the lights of Kansas City at night.

Definitely his own person, she thinks. *Confident and competent but not the least bit egotistical, and kind to everyone.*

It's the summer of 1983 in the farm town of Imperial, Nebraska, where Martin and Gracia have been head-over-heels-in-love newlyweds for less than a year. They have a great church community, Martin is working as a crop duster, and Gracia is involved in a women's Bible study and taking a class on furniture refinishing.

Martin is offered a permanent job by one of the local farmers.

One beautiful summer evening, he says to Gracia, "You know, it would be so easy to settle down in this community and make a good living, wouldn't it? . . . But that's not what we're called to do."

It's 1985 at the New Tribes Mission flight training base in Arizona, and Martin and Gracia are in a planning meeting with the mission board. "Please send us anywhere except the Philippines," Martin says. "Maybe someplace like Paraguay."

He liked the Philippines just fine, but because that's where he grew up, the old-timers in the New Tribes Mission there would remember him as just the little kid of a missionary. *Would they value his skills and respect him as a pilot? Would they feel safe trusting him with their lives when they flew with him?*

"You know, Martin," a board member says, "they really do need a replacement pilot in the Philippines. You know the culture and you partly know the language. We'd rather not send you someplace else. Would you be willing to go back?"

Gracia watches proudly as her husband nods yes. *He's just that kind of person—willing to serve wherever the call takes him.*

Anyplace will be fine with her, as long as she can be with him.

In the jungle on Mindanao, Gracia is still on the ground in the midst of the gun battle. As she crawls to Martin's side, she sees it.

Oh no! He's been hit.

From Martin's upper left chest, a growing pool of blood is soaking through his white shirt. His breathing is heavy. But he is so still that she takes her cue from him and decides not to yell for help as she normally would have.

The Filipino nurse sees him too. "Mart!" she yells. Then she is silent. She too has been struck by gunfire. She won't speak again.

31

Gracia lies quietly next to Martin, realizing their best chance to survive is to play dead so the Abu Sayyaf will flee and leave them there. The sounds of whizzing bullets and exploding grenades continue all around them.

Lord, Gracia prays, *if this is it, just make it happen quickly.*

Minutes pass as the shooting rages on. Martin moans softly a few times. Then his body slumps against hers.

The shooting subsides, then stops. She hears shouts in Tagalog, the language of the AFP, but no answering shouts from the members of Abu Sayyaf. *They must have retreated down the mountain.*

All but one of the Abu Sayyaf have escaped. From the start, the AFP had proudly denied the urgent request of the American military to take charge of a night rescue using special forces with night goggles. The Philippine government forbade the United States to intervene on its soil. Instead, the AFP went in with guns blazing in broad daylight and managed to hit all three hostages.

Gracia slowly waves her hand so the soldiers will see her without being startled—so they will not shoot anymore.

Two AFP soldiers struggle on the slippery ground to carry Gracia past the now-tattered shelter and up toward the top of the mountain, where a Black Hawk helicopter is being directed to land. She longs to make time stand still, but she can't. Looking desperately back toward Martin, she sees that the red stain now covers his chest and all color has drained from his face. There is no more breath in her husband's emaciated body.

He has gone on ahead. And she is left to hang on to the words he used to encourage her countless times: "You can do this, Gracia. You've got to go home whole."

She remembers that Martin's backpack has all the notes they wrote during their captivity and his letters to their children—memories of him that they must have.

"Go get that green bag," Gracia says. "I've got to have that. . . . You have to get it!"

32

The soldiers hesitate, but finally one goes back to retrieve it.

As a medic starts preparing her for the helicopter lift to the hospital, Gracia is suddenly so exhausted she just wants to drift off to sleep.

It's June 13, 2002, in Wichita, Kansas, six days after Martin's death. Gracia has endured a sea of concerned, caring faces at the airport, the hospital, and the American embassy in the Philippines.

She has wrestled with and defeated her bitterness against the AFP for the rescue gone wrong. By the time she met with President Arroyo of the Philippines, the venomous reproach she had contemplated had given way to a spirit of forgiveness that she knew Martin would have wanted.

Getting around in a wheelchair, Gracia has been joyously reunited with their children, and Martin's body has been returned for his funeral tomorrow.

The casket will be closed for the funeral, but it is open tonight for the family viewing. Gracia has done her best to prepare Jeffrey, Mindy, and Zach for the experience of seeing their daddy's body, now bearded and so gaunt.

In tears, they all move to the casket and say their goodbyes. Gracia knows she will miss her husband terribly—most of all, perhaps, the laughter and twinkle in his eyes, the upbeat attitude that said "no problem is ever too tough to overcome, no ordeal too grim to endure."

Gracia places her hand on his chest. *Martin. You went through so much. You were so brave, and you kept me going so I could return home. I'll always love you.*

That night, after her children are asleep and Gracia is alone, she reflects on her incredible loss and her amazing husband. She is so sad Martin is gone—and so glad that his ordeal has ended and that he's in the presence of Jesus, the Lord he served with gladness until his final breath.

Would You? Could You?

(Share your answers if you're reading in a group)

For more than a year of captivity in the jungle, Martin Burnham was able to demonstrate an attitude of Christian love—not only to his wife and fellow hostages, but also to the kidnappers who held him. He told his wife, "Jesus said that if you want to be great in God's kingdom, be the servant of all. And when he said all, he meant all. He didn't say be the servant of everyone but terrorists."

Gracia Burnham admits that she sometimes struggled with such ideas. She knew, for instance, that she should have been able to forgive her captors. "The truth is that I often hated them," she says. "I despised them not only for snatching me away from my family and the simple comforts of a life I loved, but also for forcing me to see a side of myself I didn't like . . . fearful Gracia, selfish Gracia, bitter Gracia, angry-at-God Gracia. That wasn't the only me, but it was a bigger part of me than I wanted to accept." Gracia discovered what she called "pockets of darkness" inside her.

So what's inside of you? When the superficial layers we all carry around with us are stripped away, what's left— overflowing love and goodness or ugly fear and anger? At the core, are you a servant or are you selfish? If you don't know, maybe your next crisis will help you find out.

- What if you were kidnapped by terrorists—*could you* serve and even love them the way Martin Burnham apparently did? *Would you* follow the example of the Burnhams and pray for them daily?
- Gracia says she struggled with bitterness and hate. Would *you* if you were in her shoes? Have you hated someone before? Why?
- By the time Gracia met with Philippine President Gloria Macapagal Arroyo, she had let go of the anger and bit-

terness she felt about the way her rescue was handled. *Could you* do the same? Why or why not?

- Martin was a "servant of all" in small ways—by encouraging his wife, by repairing the terrorists' satellite phone, by carrying heavy loads without complaint. Are our small acts of service just as important as our big ones? Do you serve this way when you're under stress?
- Jesus Christ washed the feet of his disciples and said, "I have set you an example that you should do as I have done for you" (John 13:15). He also said, "The Son of Man did not come to be served but to serve, and to give his life" (Matt. 20:28). How important is service in the life of a Christian?
- Muslim extremists rely on force, kidnapping, and murder to advance their cause. Gracia Burnham has written that Christians must defuse their rage and resentment through God's love. "People in today's world, whether Muslim or not, will not pay attention to Christians because we can explain our theology in crystal-clear terms," she says. "They will not esteem us because we give to charity or maintain a positive outlook on life. What will impress them is genuine love in our hearts." How can we demonstrate this love?

Reporting In

Ask the Lord to show you what is most in your heart, a spirit of servanthood or a spirit of selfishness. Then pray for him to show you how to serve him by serving others.

Hitting the Trail

(This is just for you)

You could say that Jesus Christ was a rebel. He challenged the existing order and long-held assumptions about faith and allegiance. He changed the world and inspired an ever-expanding "army" of followers—not through violence but through love.

We don't know for certain that Martin Burnham's servant attitude had an impact on the Abu Sayyaf terrorists, but we can speculate that his loving example influenced everyone who knew him well. What effect are you having on the people around you?

- List acts of service and love you've performed in the last week, whether grand or seemingly insignificant. How is your behavior challenging and changing the people in your world?

  _____

  _____

  _____

  _____

- Who serves and loves you? How do they show it? How do you respond to their actions?

  _____

  _____

  _____

- What would happen if you ramped up your commitment to serving others? Write down what you imagine would change, both in others' lives and in your own. Then pray about the idea of making it happen.

  _____

  _____

  _____

New Territory

(For those who want to explore further)

Read *In the Presence of My Enemies*, Gracia Burnham's account of her and Martin's year of terror in the jungle, and *To Fly Again*, Gracia's thoughts on the spiritual lessons she's absorbed since her captivity and release.

- In what ways would your response to kidnapping and the loss of a spouse have been the same as Gracia's? How do you think your response would have been different?
- Did God use these tragic events for good in Gracia's life? In the lives of others?

3

Dance with Death

For God so loved the world that he
gave his one and only Son.

John 3:16

In a crowded locker room at Arrowhead Pond in Anaheim, California, forty men in jeans, cowboy hats, and boots prepare to ply their unusual and dangerous trade. Some are stretching tired muscles or rubbing resin on their ropes. Others are adjusting their gloves, spurs, or mouthpieces. Some are simply sitting in front of their lockers with headphones on, lost in either their music or their own thoughts. The air is thick with off-color jokes and macho back talk, but beneath all that is something else—a growing sense of excitement and anxiety.

These men are part of what is known as the "toughest sport on dirt." They are professional bull riders. Each week, these modern-day gladiators enter a packed arena somewhere in the country to test themselves against each other and the fury of a two-thousand-pound bucking beast. Their goal is simple—to stay on an angry, writhing animal for eight full seconds. When they win, the rewards are glory, money, pride, and hero treatment. When they lose, it means no paycheck for another week—or worse.

Injuries are part of any sport, but bull riding is especially brutal on its contestants. During the finals the year before, one rider competed with a partially collapsed lung. Others were riding within weeks of suffering a broken rib, a punctured lung, or a skull fracture. The US professional rodeo circuit averages one to two deaths annually.

It is not an exercise for the timid.

On this day in Anaheim—February 14, 2004—Todd Pierce senses the tension and anticipation in the locker room. He understands it as well as anyone present. For six years, Pierce was a professional bareback horseman competing in rodeos across the country. He was one of the best, consistently ranked among the top twenty in the world.

Today, however, the thirty-three-year-old isn't a competitor. He's a pastor.

Pierce approaches a man applying tape to his gloves and claps him on the back. "Hey, how're you doing?"

"Hey, Todd," the cowboy answers with a smile.

Pierce lowers his voice. "What's been going on? How're the wife and family?"

The question is more than small talk. A career in professional bull riding can easily strain a marriage. It is a lonely as well as dangerous life. The season runs from January through November, so riders are on the road nearly all year. Young fans, many of them female, follow the riders from one venue to another as if they are rock stars. Financial pressures are ever-present for all but the most successful.

In the locker room, the cowboy with Pierce hesitates, then lowers his own voice. "Well, since you asked . . ." He launches into a discussion of a conflict he's been having with his wife.

The conversation is interrupted by a shout from one of the riders: "Let's pray!" Immediately, everyone in the room stops what they're doing. Most either bow their heads or drop to one knee.

There is a thriving Christian faction among the riders. More than a third of the tour members regularly participate in prayer meetings and Bible studies led by Pierce and others. But in the locker room, when the opportunity to meet one's maker may be only minutes away, everyone joins in.

Twenty-four-year-old Wiley Petersen stands to lead the group in prayer. Petersen is in his sixth year on the tour and is one of its rising stars. Last year he finished third in the overall standings, earning nearly $240,000.

"Dear God," Petersen says with eyes closed, "we pray for safety for everyone here today, and that you would be glorified through the things we do. We ask that we ride not only for earthly prizes but for eternal prizes, and that the people in the stands would not be just entertained but inspired."

Thirty minutes later, an announcer in a cowboy hat walks into the center of the arena. "Helloooo, Anaheim!" he yells. Fifteen thousand people yell back. It's time for some bull riding.

Pierce stays close to the action by hanging around the bucking chute where the cowboys mount their bulls. He talks to several of the riders, offering words of encouragement, and sometimes assists in their final preparations.

Pierce knows what's pulsing through their minds and veins—a thrilling mix of adrenaline, excitement, pressure, and fear. He's been drawn to rodeo-style competition since his college days at Idaho State University. Pierce was a pole-vaulter on the track team and in his spare time raced as a horse jockey. About the time he gave up both of those sports, he decided to give rodeo bareback riding a try and loved it.

Also during his years at Idaho State, Pierce experienced an even bigger life change. Though raised in a Christian home, Pierce felt he'd "outgrown" his faith by the time he reached college. During his junior year, when a staff member of Campus Crusade for Christ told him that Jesus Christ loved him and had a plan for his life, Pierce pounded the table and said, "I appreciate what you guys are doing here, but I've got to go."

Yet Pierce couldn't get the Campus Crusade staffer's words out of his head. He realized that he *did* believe in Jesus. It wasn't long before he was committing his life to Christ. Soon after, Leslie, the girlfriend who became his wife, did the same. After graduation, they concluded that God was calling them to a life in professional rodeo. Todd's fellow riders would be their mission field.

On a bucking bronco, Pierce was a natural. He was as gifted as any rider in the country. His first year, he finished third in the standings among rookie riders with the Professional Rodeo Cowboys Association. He was also a three-time Wilderness Circuit champion. Despite his talent, however, the risks of rodeo riding soon caught up with him. It started when a horse fell on him, causing a double fracture in his lower arm and leading to the insertion of a metal plate. Once that healed and Pierce was released to ride, he rebroke the same arm in a different spot. Pierce endured a year and a half of bone grafts and the reinsertion of a plate to heal this time.

Then Pierce broke a finger on his riding hand, which he rebroke two more times. That was followed by a right knee injury, which included torn anterior and posterior cruciate ligaments.

The final blow occurred at the Calgary Stampede in 2000 when Pierce reinjured the same knee. The subsequent surgery triggered the flare-up of a rare nerve disorder that eventually took him to the famous Mayo Clinic in Minnesota. When doctors told Pierce he faced at least a year of recovery time, he knew it was time to hang up his competitive spurs.

Retirement placed Pierce at a crossroads. Rodeo wasn't the most important thing in his life—God, his wife, and his family (two young boys) held that position. But his niche for serving the Lord had been sharing his faith with fellow riders on the rodeo circuit. What was he supposed to do now?

The answer began to materialize when Todd was asked to speak at a rodeo ministry event. One thing led to another; soon Todd was back on the tour—not as a competitor, but as a pastor for the Professional Bull Riders Association (PBRA). He began to see the purpose for all those injuries.

"Had I done better on a competitive level," Pierce says, "it may have been the very thing that prevented me from doing what God was calling me to do."

Back at the Anaheim Open, Pierce continues to answer the Lord's call. He's been asked to "pull rope" at the bucking chute for B. J. Kramps, a friend and fellow Christian. Kramps, at twenty-six, is a veteran of the sport and former Canadian champion.

In the tight quarters of the chute at the right corner of the arena, there's barely room for a young, tan-colored bull named Double Bogey. From outside the chute, Kramps climbs up and straddles the bull, careful to sit well back of his potentially lethal horns. The bull already has a rope around its middle. Pierce, standing on the arena side of a six-foot metal fence that separates the crowd from the arena, cinches the rope tight and hands the end to Kramps, who slips his gloved left hand under the rope and wraps the end of the rope around his hand.

Kramps nods, the chute opens, and suddenly they're in the arena, spinning and bucking together, bull and cowboy beginning their brief and violent dance with death.

Pierce watches as the bull makes three jumps and then gyrates left in a repeating spin. Kramps stays in control for the full eight seconds, his left hand secure on the rope atop Double Bogey's back, his right arm continuously lifted toward the sky. It's a strong ride, one that will merit a high score.

Pierce turns away to pull the rope for the next rider in the chute. A gasp from the crowd causes him to glance back.

Double Bogey isn't finished yet. By repeating his leftward spin, the side on which Kramps must dismount to easily untangle from the rope, he's put his rider in a pickle. When the bull keeps spinning and Kramps finally dismounts on the right, his left hand is caught in the rope.

Three bullfighters—the bull-riding equivalent of rodeo clowns, the courageous men charged with protecting fallen riders—move in. But the bull, instead of bucking and staying close, takes off running, dragging Kramps beneath him.

At the far end of the arena, the bull turns and charges back to where he started, outrunning the bullfighters. He reaches the corner of the arena at Pierce's left and then rumbles along the fence toward the bucking chute.

Pierce's gut tightens. Kramps, still being dragged, kicked, and stepped on by the bull, appears unconscious. *Oh my gosh*, Pierce thinks. *B. J.'s gettin' killed.*

The beast roars closer. Pierce doesn't stop to consider the risk, the potential to aggravate past injuries, or anything else. When Double Bogey is alongside, Pierce leaps over the bull's back and tries to grab the rope that's ensnared Kramps.

He misses.

He falls into the dirt.

The bull stops at the arena's right corner less than twenty feet away. He turns and sees Pierce.

Pierce scrambles to his feet. The three bullfighters are closing in from the middle of the arena. Kramps is still on the ground, still attached to the bull. Pierce and Double Bogey are eye to eye.

He's got nowhere to go, the pastor thinks, *but through me.*

The bull charges, head low to the ground. Pierce runs forward to meet him. Just before collision, Pierce dives above Double Bogey's head. He's trying to grab the rope and avoid those deadly horns at the same time. With help from the bull, he's flung up and over.

This time, somehow, Pierce succeeds. At the same moment, one of the bullfighters catches up and also grabs hold of the rope. Together, they quickly free Kramps.

Pierce smothers Kramps with his body to protect him from further injury. The bullfighters distract the bull. Soon the animal is corralled. The danger is past.

Pierce looks down at Kramps, fearing the worst. Kramps opens his eyes. In a typical cowboy deadpan, he says, "You can get off me now."

As far as Pierce is concerned, jumping into the arena to save a fellow rider is no big deal. "When you're filled with the love of God, your knee-jerk reaction is to go to someone's aid," he says. "When you're compelled to love, you just do it."

Kramps's extra-long ride results in a mild concussion, but no serious injuries. Later that night, after he's been patched up by a doctor, he and Pierce join other bull riders for a time of Bible study. There's no mention of the incident. It's just another day on the bull riding circuit. Right now it's time to pray. Soon enough, it will be time to prepare for the next dance with death.

Would You? Could You?

(Share your answers if you're reading in a group)

When he saw a fellow cowboy and friend in trouble, Todd Pierce didn't hesitate—he jumped in to do what he could. He put his body and even his life on the line. Though he escaped without injury, he still faced other consequences—a reprimand and a thousand-dollar fine from the PBRA. (Bull riding's powers-that-be frown on the idea of fans or even pastors joining the action in the arena.)

There's a word for what Pierce did. *Wise* isn't it. But *sacrifice* fits the bill.

Sacrifice means many things to people. Some view it as a trade-off—a mom who sacrifices her career to raise her children. Others view it as lost time—a husband who sacrifices his usual Saturday golf outing to clean out the garage. Then there are the rams and lambs presented as burnt offerings in the Old Testament. To people of faith, the purest and most loving form of sacrifice is God the Father allowing his Son to die on the cross for the sins of humanity.

So what does sacrifice mean to you? Let's get into it.

- How about it—if you were literally "on the fence," watching a friend get trampled by an angry bull, *would*

45

you jump down to help? *Could you* do anything to make a difference?

- What's your definition of sacrifice? Is it an obligation? A waste of time? A duty required by God or your spouse? An opportunity?
- What's your motivation for sacrifice? Is it a way to impress people or to get something in return? Is it love? What do you think of Todd Pierce's statement about being "compelled to love"?
- The Bible says, "This is love: not that we loved God, but that he loved us and sent his Son as an atoning sacrifice for our sins" (1 John 4:10). What is the connection between sacrifice and love?
- Does the act of sacrifice draw us closer to the Lord? Why or why not?
- Bull riders sacrifice plenty to do what they do, including their health and time with their family. Are they crazy? What do you sacrifice that others might think is crazy? Why do you do it anyway?
- Is there a price for your willingness to sacrifice? If so, what is it?

Reporting In

Sacrifice may be the ultimate act of love. Pray for the Lord's guidance in showing you how to discover that love in your heart and how to show it to others through sacrifice.

Hitting the Trail

(This is just for you)

On his last night with the disciples, Jesus said to them, "My command is this: Love each other as I have loved you. Greater love has no one than this, that he lay down his life for his friends" (John 15:12–13).

According to Christ, the willingness to give up one's life for another is an example of the greatest love of all. But can we "will" such love on our own efforts? Where does this deep love come from?

• Write down the names of people you love enough to give up your life for. Do you think God would have you expand your list?

_____

_____

_____

_____

• The apostle John wrote, "Let us love one another, for love comes from God. Everyone who loves has been born of God and knows God. Whoever does not love does not know God, because God is love" (1 John 4:7–8). Write down what this means to you.

_____

_____

_____

_____

• How can we fully embrace and understand God's love for each of us? Through reading the Bible? Prayer? Meditation? Focusing on others instead of self? List your thoughts, then ask the Lord if he is leading you to any new insights.

_____

_____

_____

New Territory

(For those who want to explore further)
Read *Fried Twinkies, Buckle Bunnies, and Bull Riders: A Year Inside the Professional Bull Riders Tour* by Josh Peter. Then attend a professional bull riding event at an arena near you.

- Bull riding has exploded in popularity. Riders compete annually for more than eleven million dollars in prize money, and over one hundred million people watch the sport in person or on TV each year. What is it that's drawing so many fans to bull riding? What's different about bull riding than other sports?
- How do bull riders on the tour sacrifice for each other?

4

The Battle for Takur Ghar

A hero is a man who does what he can.

Romain Rolland

Amid a firestorm of bullets, a Chinook helicopter lands near the top of Takur Ghar, a 10,240-foot mountain in Afghanistan. A ramp opens. Three pairs of American special operators wearing night vision goggles—five Navy SEALs and an Air Force combat controller—run into the snow. In seconds, the ramp is up and the helicopter rises into the predawn sky. The men are on their own.

This wasn't how "Slab," the team leader and a Wayne Gretzky look-alike, had planned the night's events. It is March 4, 2002, less than six months after the 9/11 terrorist attacks on America. Slab and his team, originally seven specialists, landed here two hours earlier, expecting to meet light enemy resistance. Their mission was to take control of the strategic peak as part of Operation Anaconda, an offensive against al-Qaeda and Taliban forces in the Shah-i-kot Valley.

Instead, Slab's team flew into an ambush. Before they could exit the helicopter, they were assaulted by rocket-propelled grenades, machine guns, and small arms fire. The Chinook shuddered from the attack and then jerked violently as it tried to escape. Specialist Neil "Fifi" Roberts, a thirty-two-year-old husband and father of a young son, had been on the ramp, ready to run out. He was thrown off balance. Two helicopter crewmen grabbed him. The chopper lurched again as it rose off the ground. Roberts was ripped from their grasp and fell ten feet into the snow.

They'd lost a man.

To leave a teammate behind was unthinkable. Rescuing a fallen comrade was part of the warrior code, as absolute as breathing. But when the Chinook pilot circled to return to the landing site, he found he had almost no control over the aircraft. Trying to land and lift off from the mountain would be suicide. Instead, he turned to make an emergency landing in the desert. As they flew away, a crewman spotted Roberts moving uphill, his machine gun blazing.

Now Roberts's mates are back to find him. Slab steps off the ramp into snow up to his thighs and immediately falls down. Sergeant John Chapman, the combat controller, jumps over Slab and moves toward trees near the peak. Automatic weapons and rifle fire seem to be coming from all around them.

At the high ground, Chapman discovers a bunker hidden by a canvas tarp. Chapman, thirty-six, is the married father of two daughters; even in battle, he carries a locket of hair from each of his girls. He's also an expert with an M4 carbine. At close range, he empties it into the bunker, taking out whoever's there.

Slab catches up to Chapman. Suddenly a machine gun just twenty feet away roars to life. Both Americans dive for cover, Slab behind a rock outcrop, Chapman behind a tree. Bullets fly between them.

"What do you have?" Slab shouts.

"I'm not sure!" Chapman says.

The machine gun is firing from a second bunker. Slab launches a pair of grenades at the bunker, without effect.

Chapman shoots the M4 from his knees. Slab is reloading his grenade launcher when he hears Chapman's cry: "Who did that?"

Chapman is hit. He's lying on his side, breathing, but not moving.

Slab wants to help Chapman, but first he's got to neutralize the second bunker. Two more SEALs, Brett and Kyle, are nearby. Slab plans an assault on the bunker. When the SEALs leave their cover, however, Brett is hit in the legs by bullets and pieces of a fragmentation grenade. The assault is over before it starts.

This is not working, Slab thinks. They're losing the fight. There's no sign of Roberts. They've got to get out.

Chapman no longer appears to be breathing. Slab scrambles over him and behind a tree. He wants to talk to Chapman, to feel for a pulse, but it would expose his position.

I crawled right over the top of him, Slab thinks. *I mean, you'd think he'd say something. Give me something, a grunt, a groan. Give me some sign of life. There's nothing there. There just isn't.*

The first hints of morning light are creeping along the horizon as Slab signals Randy, another SEAL, and points east. Slab throws a smoke grenade. Five SEALs retreat across an open snowfield to a ledge near the top of the mountain. Turbo, the last team member, suddenly shouts and goes down. Randy drags him to a tree stump near the ledge. One of Turbo's legs has nearly been amputated above the ankle.

"Where's Chappy?" Randy asks.

"He's dead," Slab says.

Soon, enemy fighters are shooting down at the SEALs from the peak. Then al-Qaeda mortars begin pounding the mountainside. The would-be rescuers need rescue themselves.

An Air Force Spectre gunship, piloted by Major D. J. Turner, makes strafing runs across the peak, giving the SEALs some protection. But the gunship is a nighttime weapon. With dawn breaking, the Spectre is a fat target for al-Qaeda or Taliban with surface-to-air missiles. The rule book says they should be out of harm's way at thirty minutes to daylight.

51

On his radio, Turner hears orders to go home. A different commander orders him to stay on the scene. Officers begin a heated discussion. Turner hears that a quick response force is on its way, but it's not due for another hour or two.

Turner stays. He's not abandoning the SEALs while he still has fuel. The minutes pass. The sun rises. Commanders argue over the radio. The Spectre's fuel gauges drop lower.

Finally, after disobeying orders for an hour, Turner feels he has no choice. He's got a two-hour flight home and less than thirty minutes of leeway fuel to get there. The Spectre makes one last sweep and disappears into the morning sky.

Captain Nate Self, a twenty-five-year-old Texan, is leading a team of Army Rangers and Air Force Special Tactics forces. Counting its crew, twenty-one men are in a Chinook helicopter headed toward Takur Ghar. But Self is confused. A radio has failed and communication with their base is garbled. He thinks they're supposed to meet and pick up SEALs and the "guy who fell out" on an earlier mission, but he and the pilots have received multiple grid locations. He's not sure where they're landing or where the SEALs are located.

Pilot Al Calvert has to choose a landing site. He decides on the mountain's top. At 6 a.m., the Chinook roars to the peak and begins descending to a nearly level area surrounded by rock.

At fifty feet above the ground, a spray of bullets slams into the cockpit. Two strike Calvert's helmet. Eight more hit the Kevlar armor on his chest.

Calvert starts to pull up, but his left engine has been hit by an RPG (rocket propelled grenade) and isn't working. He doesn't have the power. He has to land. When he does, hard, the Chinook is a sitting duck. They are being attacked on all four sides, including from the same bunkers that the SEALs encountered earlier, fifty meters away. In the first fifteen seconds, a Ranger and a crewman are killed on the chopper, and two more Rangers are shot dead when they run down the ramp. Many more are wounded.

More of the remaining Rangers exit the Chinook and find whatever cover they can. Self, at the helicopter's ramp, is struck in the thigh by shrapnel from an exploding RPG. He's too amped to pay it much attention.

We are going to be here all day long, he thinks. *The sun is just coming up. It's not over the mountains yet. This aircraft is not taking off again. We are in the middle of a fight. There is no way out of it.*

He runs for a section of rock three feet high and fires three or four rounds from his M4. Then a round jams inside the weapon. Self tries to push it out with his cleaning rod, but the rod breaks. He runs to the Chinook, grabs the M4 of a dead Ranger, and scrambles back to his cover position.

Gabe Brown, an Air Force combat controller behind Self, makes radio contact with the SEALs below the ridge. Neither group can help the other. Slab's team is wounded and in no condition to climb back up the mountain. Self's men are pinned down and fighting for their lives.

Self considers an assault on the peak. Unless they can take the high ground, they'll never have the advantage. Two F-15E fighter jets arrive to assist, and Self orders a strafing run on the bunkers and trees nearby. Then he hears mortars launching from behind them. The first round lands just ten feet in front of the Chinook.

We can't just sit here and take mortar rounds, Self thinks. *We've got to assault.*

Self notices movement in the sky. It's a CIA Predator, the twenty-seven-foot-long unmanned reconnaissance craft that resembles a model airplane.

"Find out if the Predator is armed!" he shouts to Brown.

"What are you talking about?" Brown says. "It's just a Predator."

"Nope. Some of 'em are armed. Ask the question."

Moments later, Self hears the first good news he's had since the attack began: "They got two Hellfires."

Self orders a strike on the bunkers above. The first fourteen-pound warhead misses. The second is a hit, destroying a tree and a barrier of logs in front of the first bunker. Some of the Rangers cheer.

It's time to move. Self and three Rangers begin firing weapons and advancing through the snow toward the bunkers. The thin air and slippery surface make for slow going. Some of the Rangers briefly drop to one knee and gulp for air.

Self sees a guerilla behind the logs at the bunker. One of the advancing Rangers fires on the position. Self can't see the enemy now, but he's nervous. His team still has twenty-five meters to go. They're moving too slowly. One sweeping burst from the bunker could wipe them out.

"Get back! Get back! Get back!" Self calls off the assault. The Rangers scramble back to their original positions.

To the south, help is on its way. Lower on Takur Ghar, a Chinook has dropped off the second half of what was originally planned as a two-pronged quick response force led by Self. Ten Rangers are completing a two-thousand-foot climb to the peak. As they flew in, they recited the Ranger creed: "Surrender is not a Ranger word. I will never leave a fallen comrade to fall into the hands of the enemy."

At close to 11 a.m., the second group of Rangers links with Self's team. One of the new Rangers is Sergeant Eric Stebner, wearing only boots, camouflage pants, and a T-shirt. He'd anticipated a mission in the desert.

When they arrive, Stebner notices an American helmet in the snow. Someone has written the name "Fifi" on it. The helmet has bullet holes in the front and back.

Self plans a new assault with his enlarged team. He's worried about taking the most strategic position on the mountain and about evacuating the wounded. Some, he knows, are in bad shape.

A few minutes later, the Rangers are in position. Self radios Staff Sergeant Arin Canon: "Okay, we're ready for you to initiate."

"Well, what's the signal?" Canon asks.

"Shoot. Start shootin'."

The assault is over in just a few minutes. During the attack, the Rangers shoot the only remaining enemy guerilla at the bunkers and another on the other side of the hill. The rest are already dead.

The Rangers find two other bodies at the top of the mountain: Neil Roberts, lying in the snow just feet away from the first bunker, and John Chapman, buried under debris in the bunker. There's nothing more the Rangers can do for them. The wounded, however, are another matter. Self orders that they be carried up to the relative safety of the bunkers.

They're too late. Stebner and another Ranger are dragging wounded Chinook crewman Sergeant Dave Dube up the slope on a stretcher when al-Qaeda reinforcements from the south begin a counterattack with RPGs, machine guns, and AK-47s. Stebner and the other Ranger dive for cover behind a rock. Dube is in the open.

"Don't worry, sergeant, we're coming to get you!" Stebner shouts.

"You don't have to!" Dube says. "You fight!"

During what seems a lull in the shooting, Stebner dashes from his position and pulls Dube uphill a few yards. When the bullets start flying again, Stebner takes cover.

Dube tries to get up. Stebner runs into the open again and pulls Dube farther. There's forty feet to go. Then more bullets send Stebner scrambling for cover. "They don't like me!" Stebner says to another Ranger. "Every time I get up they shoot at me."

Stebner runs out a third time, the snow around him kicking up from the impact of bullets, and finally drags Dube over the crest to safe cover.

A few minutes later, Navy fighter jets drop bombs into the al-Qaeda ranks. Though sporadic gunfire continues, the counterattack, and the battle for Takur Ghar, is over.

Stebner, freezing and barely able to walk, makes his way to the downed Chinook and finds a friend on his back in the snow, staring up at the sky. He closes his friend's eyes.

It's not until evening that helicopters arrive to take Slab and Self's men from the scene of so much destruction. Exhausted Rangers load seven dead, including the bodies of Roberts and Chapman, into a Chinook.

Everyone is accounted for. They're going home.

Would You? Could You?

(Share your answers if you're reading in a group)

The Ranger vow to "never leave a fallen comrade to fall into the hands of the enemy" is a concept that was stated in different words during biblical times. Jesus once said, "Suppose one of you has a hundred sheep and loses one of them. Does he not leave the ninety-nine in the open country and go after the lost sheep until he finds it? And when he finds it, he joyfully puts it on his shoulders and goes home. Then he calls his friends and neighbors together and says, 'Rejoice with me; I have found my lost sheep'" (Luke 15:4–6). It is an idea based on brotherhood and love.

The men involved in the escalating events on Takur Ghar in 2002 were committed to this philosophy. From the moment that Neil Roberts fell out of the Chinook and onto the mountain, their ironclad belief in the need to find their "lost sheep" led them to heroic and deadly decisions. According to video feeds from the Predator, Roberts ascended the mountain alone and reached a pine tree near the first bunker. He fell there; he'd been wounded and could no longer move. Minutes later, al-Qaeda guerillas emerged from the bunkers and found Roberts. He may already have been dead. If not, one of the guerillas made sure of it, putting a single bullet from an AK-47 into his head at 4:27 a.m.

The SEALs and Rangers who later landed on Takur Ghar didn't know whether Roberts was dead or alive. In one sense, it didn't matter. Either way, they were going to retrieve their brother and fellow warrior. No matter what it took, they would bring him home.

- As soon as Roberts fell into the snow on Takur Ghar, his chances of survival were slim. *Would you* risk your life and the lives of others to rescue a man who had little chance to live? *Could you* go into battle against a well-armed enemy with superior numbers?
- From a tactical standpoint, how wise is it to commit men and resources to a "lost cause"? If you were in command of Operation Anaconda, would you have authorized a rescue attempt on Takur Ghar?
- Major D. J. Turner, circling in the Spectre gunship, refused Slab's request for support fire before the SEALs' second landing, fearing it might kill Roberts. Later, Turner disobeyed orders to protect Slab and his team. Do you agree with Turner's decisions? Why or why not?
- Communications and weaponry did not always function as desired or needed during the battle for Takur Ghar. It probably cost some Americans their lives. As a society, what do we gain from our reliance on technology? What do we lose? Does our faith have anything to say about this?
- Ranger Eric Stebner put himself at risk three times to save a helicopter crewman. One fellow Ranger thought it was the most heroic thing he'd ever seen. Do you agree? Would you have done what Stebner did?
- The duties of American servicemen and women sometimes include the killing of enemies. Is this godly? When is it appropriate to fight and when is it not? How do followers of Christ reconcile warfare with Jesus's admonition to turn the other cheek (Matt. 5:38–42)?

Reporting In

Jesus clearly has passion for his lost children. Do you share his passion? Ask him to show you what the parable of the lost sheep means for your life.

Hitting the Trail

(This is just for you)

Even in an organization as structured as the military, the officers and enlisted men fighting in the battle for Takur Ghar often found themselves making decisions based on their values and instincts instead of following direct orders. No one instructed Eric Stebner to attempt a rescue of Dave Dube. D. J. Turner actually disregarded orders to return to base.

Even when we don't think we have a choice, we usually do. God has given us the authority to make our own choices, if only we'll use it.

- Are you feeling trapped by any circumstances in your life? Write down what the consequences would be if you choose what seems impossible. If the "impossible" seems to fit within God's plan for your life, maybe it's time to make a radical decision.

_____

_____

_____

- Who are the "lost sheep" in your world? Are you actively doing anything to serve or help them? If not, why not?

_____

_____

_____

- Read Joshua 24:15. Deep down, who or what do you choose to serve on a daily basis? Write down all of your "gods" and decide if you need to make any changes to your list.

_____

_____

_____

New Territory

(For those who want to explore further)

Read *Roberts Ridge*, Malcolm MacPherson's retelling of the 2002 battle on Takur Ghar, and *Not a Good Day to Die*, Sean Naylor's account of Operation Anaconda.

- Was Operation Anaconda a success or a mistake? Why?
- What is it that Navy SEALs and Army Rangers have that allows them to succeed at what they do? How many of these qualities or abilities do you possess?

PART TWO

PERSEVERANCE

5

Cold Night in the Elk Mountains

We consider blessed those who have persevered.

James 5:11

At the start, I didn't think a bit about hypothermia or desperate thirst or whether I'd see my wife again. I was with friends on an adventure. That was what mattered.

It was all Dick Savidge's idea. He'd called me a couple of weeks before at my office in Glendora, California. "Peb!" he'd said. "Let's go get scared." Dick and I had been partners in crime before: ice climbs and a summit of the Petit Grepon in Rocky Mountain National Park; adventures with Tim Hansel's Summit Expedition outfit; and ice climbs in Vail, including the day Dick broke his leg on the treacherous Rigid Designator. The idea this time was to cross-country ski through twenty miles of snow country over a pass into Aspen. Dick knew I was ready for any chance to test my limits.

That's how we found ourselves standing at a trailhead near Crested Butte, Colorado, on a January morning in 1989:

Dick, a former Outward Bound instructor from Denver; Stevan Strain, a restaurant owner and Himalayan climber from Colorado Springs; Bill, a Colorado carpenter and alpine-style climber; and me, Peb Jackson, an outdoorsman who was always looking for an excuse to return to the elements. It was 4 a.m. The night was bold and black, the stars intense from our vantage point at about eight thousand feet. It was also twenty degrees below zero, a "snap, crackle, and pop" cold.

Our intention was to cross-country ski to another trailhead in Aspen, more than twenty miles northeast as the crow flies. The terrain was difficult, a series of passes and ridges and slopes. We'd never heard of anyone making the journey in a single day. But we were all in great shape and confident of our abilities in the outdoors—maybe too confident. We wore insulated long underwear and several layers of clothing but carried no tents or sleeping bags, no down of any kind. We had no stove. Our food supply consisted of energy bars and water bottles. The plan was to travel light and fast and arrive in Aspen by dark.

That was the plan.

I was enthralled during those first hours. Despite having to break trail through heavy snow, we made good progress along an old jeep trail. The only sounds were of ice and twigs crackling beneath our skis and our own breathing. The crisp air froze inside my nose and throat. Even in the extreme cold, I quickly worked up a sweat.

A couple of hours into the journey, the first hints of a gorgeous sunrise appeared over the top of the Elk Mountains ahead of us. It was an amazing sight: a blanket of pristine snow, endless spires of evergreen trees that cast long black shadows, and an overcoat of orange rays draped across the landscape. We were surrounded by stark beauty.

"Dick," I huffed as we hiked, "we've been a lot of places together. I love this environment. It's primal territory."

"Peb, that's exactly why I call you," Dick replied. "You're always game."

It was midmorning when we reached a small wooden sign etched with the words "Pearl Pass" and an arrow pointing left.

This was the landmark we were looking for. We consulted our crude map to confirm our bearings, but its lack of detail provided little help. We turned in the direction of the arrow and pushed on, continuing to sink with our skis into heavy powder past our knees with each step.

Only later did we learn our mistake. Pearl Pass was actually dead ahead. Something or someone had turned the sign. We were heading into unknown territory.

A couple of hours later, Stevan was breaking trail, and I was second in line. Stevan glanced over his shoulder at me and without stopping said, "You know, something's not quite right here. We should be at the pass by now."

"You're right," I said. "But we'll get out of here." I knew that once we got over Pearl Pass, it was a straight shot to Aspen. Yet for the first time, I felt a tug of concern. As the sun dropped lower in the sky, my concern grew.

It was late afternoon when we reached the upper end of a cirque. Beyond it was the top of what we thought was Pearl Pass. This steep gulley, however, was not a place we wanted to be. It looked ripe for an avalanche. Yet to go higher was impossible; it was too steep. Turning around was equally unappealing. We were twelve hours and many miles into the journey. We also knew that Dick's wife was waiting alone for us at the Aspen trailhead. In these days before cell phones, we had no way of contacting her.

We gathered in a small huddle. Despite the subzero temperature, I was hot from the exertion and terribly thirsty. I pulled a water bottle from inside my jacket, where I'd placed it long before in hopes of melting it. No luck—the water was still frozen. Next I tried an energy bar. It too was frozen, but I was able to bite off a small piece to chew.

We weighed the alternatives. "I still don't know exactly where the heck we are," Stevan said, "but I've got to believe that if we can get across this slope and over the pass, the hike to Aspen shouldn't be too bad."

Bill looked behind us. "I don't want to go back now," he said. "We'd be hiking all night." He surveyed the slope in front of us, then turned to Dick and me. "What do you guys think? It looks a little dicey, but we don't have much choice. Are you up for moving ahead?"

According to the Colorado Avalanche Information Center, avalanches kill about twenty-five people in the United States each year, including six per annum in Colorado. The most dangerous are slab avalanches, which occur when stronger snow overlies weaker snow. A single man disturbing this perilous terrain is enough to ignite a massive shift in the landscape. In seconds, a slope as long as half a football field can simply disappear.

"We've got to do this," Dick said. "But we've got to be really careful."

I took a deep breath. I also took consolation in knowing these guys were experienced climbers. I trusted their judgment.

"Let's get going," I said. "I'm getting cold."

The field in front of us was about a hundred yards across and far too steep for us to stop ourselves if we fell, especially without ice axes. Below it was a drop of several hundred feet. It might as well have been ten thousand.

Stevan would go first. He took off his skis and strapped them on his back. He would kick steps across the slope, using his poles for balance as he moved. There was no point in roping up—if one of us fell, he'd take the rest with him. Stevan began gingerly picking his way across the slope while the rest of us held our breath.

Less than an hour later, Stevan and Dick were safely across. It was my turn. *Lord*, I prayed, *give me energy. Keep me safe. Help me to keep my focus.* I stepped onto the slope and felt the snow compact beneath my boots. I was grateful that Stevan had kicked in a trail. I tried to will myself to be as light as possible.

A couple years earlier, I'd been crossing a similar stretch of snow at the Maroon Bells near Aspen. I was about twenty yards into the slope, carefully checking each step but trying to move at a steady pace, when a friend behind me called out,

"Peb, don't even think about it. Just go." I heard the urgency in his voice. What he wasn't telling me was that a crack in the snow had just opened up behind me. Thankfully, that one didn't develop into a slab avalanche. I'm not sure to this day why it didn't.

This time, I didn't waste energy looking around. I kept my eyes straight ahead and focused on making progress. I couldn't afford to let my mind drift. This was the ultimate moment for paying close attention. I gave myself to the rhythm of it—step to the right, place the pole, adjust for balance, breathe. Do it all again.

It felt as if time stood still.

Yet with each step and breath, time did pass. Twenty minutes later, I was across.

By the time Bill joined us, it was nearly dark. Grateful to still be alive and together, we climbed up the rocky incline that led to a ridge. Finally, after some thirteen hours of hiking, we reached the top of a pass—though not the one we were looking for. From Pearl Pass, we would have seen the lights of cabins. Here, there was nothing ahead of us but blackness. Only later did we learn it was Triangle Pass, thirteen thousand feet above sea level and at least two miles to the west of our intended goal.

I remembered the time that Dick and I thought we were climbing the Petit Grepon until we realized the route was much tougher than we anticipated. Somehow we'd gotten on the wrong face. We'd had to rappel off in the rain—Dick fell once—then hike out for seven miles.

How do we get into these things? I wondered.

We put on skis again and in the darkness picked our way through rocks and steep grades. At one point, Bill's binding broke. We had to jury-rig a repair job.

I was exhausted and dehydrated. I hadn't had a drink since early in our trek. I felt a hot spot at the bottom of my right foot, but didn't realize then that my sock was filling with blood where my skin had rubbed raw against the heel of my boot.

We'd already taken one wrong turn. In the back of my mind, I acknowledged a growing awareness of the consequences if we made another wrong decision. We couldn't stop because we didn't have the gear to survive a night in these conditions. I was grateful to be going downhill after so many hours going up, but I was also feeling wasted.

I knew that the secret to covering a long distance was to focus on small objectives. On the way up, I'd thought, *I'll just get to that next boulder. It's only a hundred yards.* One step at a time, we were creating a mosaic in the snow, small strips of trail that would form what we hoped was our deliverance.

We each wore headlamps that brought small comfort in the deepening darkness. For the next two hours, we skied close together and focused on avoiding rocks. A broken ankle here would be seriously bad news. I concentrated on trying to stay upright.

Suddenly, Bill's voice cut through the night: "You guys smell something?"

I sniffed. "Smells like smoke," I said, improbable as that sounded.

A minute later, I could make out a black mass roughly thirty yards away and illuminated by flickering light from within. How could something be on fire out here? As we approached, I could see that it was a broken-down miner's cabin.

With newfound hope, we hurried to the "door" of the tiny cabin—an old rug hanging over the opening—and peeked inside. To our amazement, a man and woman were sitting there in sleeping bags. They were brewing up a small pot of tea and huddled close to a couple of logs burning in a fire pit.

"Mind if we join you?" Stevan asked.

The couple looked so startled that words failed them for a moment. "Where did you guys come from?" the woman finally said.

"Crested Butte."

"You're kidding."

We stumbled into the small space and stood there with silly grins on our faces. The joy of that moment is impossible to relate. To find an oasis and human contact in this primitive place was a gift beyond what we'd hoped for.

Still, our relief was tempered by the news that we were a good six miles from Aspen, and we had to push on. Even if we'd had a way to stay warm overnight, there wasn't room for six of us here. We enjoyed a few sips of tea, the first liquid to reach our parched lips for many hours, and chewed on a few bites of granola. Then we slipped on our skis and stepped back into the dark woods. It all happened so quickly that it didn't seem real.

Even though we were going downhill, it still required maximum effort. My legs felt like sticks. I knew I didn't have much left. I concentrated on keeping a rhythm: *Left. Right. Breathe.*

A couple of hours later, Dick's voice broke the stillness of the night: "Look."

I glanced up. Perhaps a mile distant were a few yellow pinpricks. They were the lights of cabins. It meant people, civilization, and rest were not far away.

Those lights were like a beacon during the final stage of our arduous journey. I recalled the words of John about Christ: "What came into existence was Life, and the Life was Light to live by. The Life-Light blazed out of the darkness; the darkness couldn't put it out" (John 1:4–5 Message).

It was probably after midnight, more than twenty hours since our departure, when we dragged ourselves to the front door of one of the cabins on the outskirts of Aspen. We would have been a frightening sight—four exhausted men, icicles hanging from our beards, barely able to stand up. But we didn't care. We'd made it.

When a man opened the door, we all stared at each other for a few moments. In a raspy, barely audible voice, I finally got out the words that needed to be said.

"Would you please call for a taxi?"

Would You? Could You?

(Share your answers if you're reading in a group)
"Alpine style" is a mountaineering term for the idea of bringing what is necessary and nothing more—traveling light and fast to the summit. It means less exposure to the risks of avalanche and weather, but also less margin for error. Herman Buhl was among the first to employ these tactics on high peaks in the 1950s. Two decades later, Reinhold Messner and Peter Habeler popularized the style, starting with the summit of the Himalayan peak Gasherbrum I in 1975. Messner eventually became the first man to summit Everest without supplemental oxygen in 1978.

This was the approach our (Peb's) team had in mind when we set out for Aspen that cold day in 1989. We were confident in our outdoor skills. By foregoing overnight gear, we planned to move quickly and arrive in Aspen by nightfall. The problem, of course, was that our wrong turn left us vulnerable to nature's icy grip. In retrospect, a stove would have been nice!

For some of us, alpine style is more than a method of climbing or cross-country skiing. It's a way of life. We set aside precautions others cling to and push hard and fast for the goal. It's a thrilling existence, one that frequently leads to the razor-thin edge between success and disaster.

How close to the edge are *you* willing to go to achieve your goals?

- *Would you* put yourself at risk to ski without overight gear across the Elk Mountains, as these men did? *Could you* have persevered when it became obvious the plan had gone awry?
- Should they have turned around at the avalanche field?
- What level of risk should people strive for in outdoor pursuits: Low? Medium? High? What about in business?

How about other areas of life such as relationships and family?

- How can we tell the difference between a foolhardy risk and one that is going to help us grow?
- Dick Savidge's invitation to the Aspen adventure began with the line, "Let's go get scared." Why are so many of us attracted to the idea of being scared? Is this healthy or not? Does it help us value the gift of life? Does it help us understand the Bible's admonition to "Fear the LORD your God" (Deut. 6:13)?
- Peb said that "the secret to covering a long distance was to focus on small objectives." Is this true in all aspects of life? What are some examples?
- When we persevere in other areas of life, does this also strengthen our ability to persevere in faith and service to the Lord?

Reporting In

Scripture says, "We consider blessed those who have persevered" (James 5:11). Are you persevering in your faith through hard times or difficult journeys? Thank the Lord for his blessing and ask him for guidance and strength.

Hitting the Trail

(This is just for you)

The life of faith is a daring adventure, full of risk and danger. Jesus said, "Risk your life and get more than you ever dreamed of. Play it safe and end up holding the bag" (Luke 19:26 Message). The problem is that many of us *are* playing it safe. We rest in our comfortable routine, never asking the Lord if he wants more of us.

Let's take a closer look at the purpose and meaning of risk.

71

- Make two lists—one of potential benefits to taking risks and the other of potential drawbacks. Include examples from your life.

  _____

  _____

  _____

  _____

- Write down examples from Scripture of people who took risks for their faith. Now add people you know personally to the list. Does your name belong on the list?

  _____

  _____

  _____

  _____

- Write down any risks that the Lord might be asking you to consider today. What is holding you back from moving ahead? Pray about it.

  _____

  _____

  _____

New Territory

(For those who want to explore further)

Read *The Worst Journey in the World*, Apsley Cherry-Garrard's retelling of Robert Scott's doomed expedition to the South Pole, and *The Crystal Horizon*, Reinhold Messner's account of the first solo ascent of Everest.

- What enabled Scott and Messner to persevere despite incredible obstacles? Did their goals (especially considering the deaths of Scott and his men) justify the risk?
- How would you describe the quality and character of these men? Are these qualities admirable or something to be avoided? Why?

6

Sailing for Glory

Everything can be found at sea,
according to the spirit of your quest.

Joseph Conrad

Robin Knox-Johnston awakens to darkness, a roaring in his ears, and blows striking his prone body.

The thumping stops, and he lies still a moment to gather his wits. Right—he is on his ketch, the *Suhaili*, in a gale-force storm on the Southern Ocean. It's the middle of the night, and the storm has apparently tossed his small sailing ship onto its side, dumping the contents of the cabin on top of him in the process.

And, of course, he is utterly alone.

It is September 3, 1968. Knox-Johnston is one of nine participants in one of the most daring races ever attempted. The objective? To be the first to sail solo around the world—without stopping in any port and without help of any kind. No one has ever done it.

The previous year, one man came close. England's Francis Chichester, owner of a book and map store in London, circumnavigated the globe in a thirty-nine-foot sloop. He stopped just once, in Australia. The effort brought worldwide attention to sailing and to Chichester, who was knighted by Queen Elizabeth II. For sailing enthusiasts, only one grand achievement remains—a nonstop solo circuit.

The race is sponsored by London's *Sunday Times* newspaper. The first to return after circling the world will receive a trophy, the "Golden Globe." In addition, whoever records the fastest time will earn a cash prize of £5,000. Fame, honor, and additional wealth are likely to follow.

Knox-Johnston is, in many ways, an unlikely contender. At twenty-eight, he is the second-youngest competitor, less experienced than several of his rivals. They include Bernard Moitessier, a Frenchman famous for his nonstop voyage from Tahiti to Spain; Bill King, former British Navy submarine commander; Nigel Tetley, a Royal Navy lieutenant commander; and English electronics engineer Donald Crowhurst, who reportedly sails on a trimaran with a revolutionary design.

As for Knox-Johnston, many people, himself included, feel his boat is wrong for a winning effort. *Suhaili*, made of heavy Indian teak and forty-four feet long, is not built for speed. It resembles a tugboat more than a yacht. It was not his first choice. He had a longer, sleeker boat designed but couldn't raise the funds to build it.

Yet Knox-Johnston does bring attributes to the race. He is a captain in the British Merchant Marines, well schooled in classic sailing techniques. And he knows his boat well; he has already sailed *Suhaili* from India to London (with two crew members and several stops along the way).

Of course, a solo voyage of some ten months around the world is quite another matter. Before departing, Knox-Johnston wondered if he was up to it. Could he stand not having anyone to talk to for nearly a year? A sociable man, the longest he'd been on his own was twenty-four hours.

This was a voluntary sentence of solitary confinement, hard labor, and constant danger. Perhaps he would go mad. It had happened before on the high seas.

But Knox-Johnston, along with the other racers, had quickly realized that the obstacles, hardships, and threat to his life did not matter. He was a stubborn patriot, and he feared that the French would grab all the glory. He'd already made up his mind. He was going.

Nearly three months after his launch, during the storm on the Southern Ocean, Knox-Johnston has reason to question his decision. Waking up in the darkness, pinned against his bunk by boxes, tools, tins, and who-knows-what, he can barely move.

With significant effort, Knox-Johnston emerges from the weights that imprison him, only to be immediately flung to the other side of the cabin when *Suhaili* lurches upright again. He fights through the dark and debris to the companionway and then to the deck, fearing the worst: torn sails, tangled wires, and masts turned to stumps.

On deck, the wind howls fiercely and spray fills the air; Knox-Johnston can taste saltwater on his lips. He has to blink in the near-total darkness before he believes it: the masts are intact. *Suhaili* has not escaped unscathed—one of the two wind vanes crucial to self-steering is badly bent and jammed—but he is pleased the damage isn't worse.

Knox-Johnston continues to feel his way around the deck, making sure each piece of rigging is tight. He's nearly returned to his starting point when another rogue wave smashes into him. He hangs on for his life as a wall of water cascades over him.

He alters course slightly, then goes below. There he is alarmed to discover large cracks around the edge of the cabin; the interior bulkheads have shifted. Another knockdown could rip the entire cabin off, leaving Knox-Johnston—if he survives the separation—entirely vulnerable in the middle of a tempest. Despite the risk, however, there is little he can do about it until the storm subsides and daylight returns. A practical man, Knox-Johnston swallows a shot of whiskey, wraps himself in canvas, and goes to sleep.

When he awakens, the fury of the wind and waves has lessened. After a breakfast of porridge, coffee, and a cigarette, he feels "quite happy." Over the next two days, Knox-Johnston is able to make effective repairs and continue toward the southern tip of Africa and the Cape of Good Hope. By mid-November he is past the middle leg in the journey, Australia's Cape Leeuwin. He is, in fact, leading the race, though Moitessier and others are closing on him. All that remains is the final and most formidable passage: South America and the dreaded Cape Horn.

At this same time, another Golden Globe racer faces a far different crisis. Crowhurst, the electronics engineer, was described by the *Times* as a "mystery competitor." Intelligent and technically skilled, he had devised several nautical innovations, including a direction-finding instrument called the Navicator. Sales were slow, however, and his business, Electron Utilisation, was struggling. A consummate optimist with a buoyant personality, Crowhurst saw the race as an opportunity to demonstrate the effectiveness of his innovations and revitalize his business.

The thirty-five-year-old husband and father of four wagered everything on the voyage. To raise funds for building a trimaran, he signed an agreement with a business associate. If Crowhurst did not complete the voyage, he would have to pay back the cost of the boat. Later, in need of more funds, he signed a second agreement with the associate, taking out a second mortgage on his home. If Crowhurst did not turn in a tremendous showing, he was ruined financially.

Crowhurst and his *Teignmouth Electron* were towed out of the harbor in Teignmouth on October 31, the deadline for departure. When he tried to raise sails, however, he found they'd been improperly placed. Crowhurst was ignominiously towed back to the dock for a quick repair.

78

Now, two weeks later, Crowhurst is for the first time facing the awful truth: his boat is in no condition for a round-the-world voyage. The boatbuilders, in their haste to meet the race deadline, have done a poor job. The steering gear has been badly installed. The port hull and cockpit floor hatch are leaking, and tools and supplies needed for repairs are missing. His radio is malfunctioning. Seawater has soaked his generator. And the "computer" that Crowhurst had promised to invent to power one of his innovations, a self-righting buoyancy bag, is unfinished.

Crowhurst keenly feels the weight he now carries, much of it his own fault. His family is depending on him. He argues the pros and cons of the dilemma in his logbook. To give up now will result in shame and bankruptcy. Yet to continue appears pointless at best, and probably life-threatening. "Racked by the growing awareness that I must soon decide whether or not I can go on in the face of the actual situation," he writes in his logbook. "What a bloody awful decision—to chuck it in at this stage—what a bloody awful decision!"

Soon after, Crowhurst stops recording his tormented thoughts. He sails almost in a circle, and from a pilot book even draws a detailed map of a Portugal harbor, apparently for the purpose of landing there. But on November 22 he sails southwest, moving at speed again. He has made a decision. Crowhurst has found a third option.

On December 6, Crowhurst opens a new logbook and continues to track his true position there. In the old logbook—still half empty—he begins listing a new series of positions. They are fabrications. And with each passing day, they show him farther and farther from his actual location in the Atlantic. On December 15, thanks to repairs on his radio, the *Sunday Times* reports to the world that Crowhurst is moving rapidly—and that on December 10, he covered 243 miles in a single day, thought to be a sailing record. The *Times* has no way to verify Crowhurst's data.

On Christmas Eve, still in the Atlantic, Crowhurst is able to make a radiotelephone call to his wife, Clare. The children miss their father terribly, there has been a fire next to his workshop, and the business is generating so little money that the family is nearly desperate. Yet Clare mentions none of this to her husband; she does not want to worry him. He, in turn, tells her that all is well.

Knox-Johnston, meanwhile, enjoys his solitary Christmas Eve. After two glasses of whiskey, he climbs on top of his cabin and belts out a series of Christmas carols. He ends the day feeling "quite merry."

The merchant marine captain is approaching Cape Horn and still leading the race, but thanks to a message he receives off the coast of New Zealand, he knows that Moitessier is gaining on him. The *Times* predicts a photo finish in April. Knox-Johnston pushes *Suhaili* as hard as he dares.

On January 17, through clearings between manageable squalls, he spots the Horn's outlying islands, as well as mountain ranges topped with glacial ice. That evening, after another squall clears, he spies Cape Horn itself. He is already past. Knox-Johnston writes "Yippee!!!" in his logbook and adjusts his course for home.

Can anyone predict how a man will react to months alone at sea? In the case of Bernard Moitessier, he is poised to possibly win both the Golden Globe trophy and the cash prize for fastest circumnavigation. He can become the most famous yachtsman in the world. Yet he fears, even loathes, what fame and wealth could do to him. He realizes that the happiest days of his life have not been not on land but aboard his vessel in the vast open space of the oceans.

On March 18, after passing Cape Horn, Moitessier slingshots a canister aboard a tanker ship. It contains a message for the *Times*, declaring his intention to drop out of the race and keep sailing toward the Pacific. "I am continuing nonstop because I am happy at sea," he writes, "and perhaps because I want to save my soul."

On April 12, Knox-Johnston hears the astonishing news about Moitessier. Just ten days later, he enters the harbor at Falmouth, accompanied by a fleet of boats containing media representatives and well-wishers. Knox-Johnston waves to the crowds. A cannon fires and people on boats and ashore cheer. Moments later, British customs officials board *Suhaili*, its first visitors in almost a year. The senior officer, trying to keep a straight face, performs his mandatory duty. "Where from?" he asks. Knox-Johnston replies, "Falmouth."

After 313 days and more than thirty thousand miles, the long battle is over. Knox-Johnston has won the great race. Like Chichester, he is knighted. He writes a bestselling book about his adventure and is showered with honorary degrees and maritime awards.

Some of his rivals are less fortunate.

On May 20, Nigel Tetley is near the Azores, only about a thousand miles from England. He has been pushing his trimaran to its breaking point, knowing he has a chance to win the prize for fastest time and believing that Crowhurst is close behind and gaining. That night, in the midst of a strong gale, he is awakened by a scraping, wracking sound in the bow. The port hull has broken away, and in the process has smashed a hole in the bow of the main hull. His boat is sinking. Tetley radios a mayday, jumps into a life raft, and is rescued the next afternoon.

Only later does Tetley discover that Crowhurst was actually nowhere near his position, that he needn't have pushed so hard and still might have captured the speed record. The disappointment gnaws at him. In the years that follow, Tetley has a new boat built with the intention of breaking the solo circumnavigation record. Despite repeated attempts, however, he fails to attract a sponsor to fund outfitting the voyage. On February 5, 1972, Nigel Tetley is found hanging from a tree near Dover.

As for Crowhurst, he learns of Tetley's sinking on May 23. He is now the only competitor in the race. If Tetley had finished and beaten Crowhurst's supposed time, the logbooks of the *Teignmouth Electron* might have escaped close scrutiny. Now, however, he knows that every scribble of his fabrications will be carefully checked.

Crowhurst allows his boat to drift. In stifling heat, he works on his radio, which has failed again. He has time—too much time—to consider his dilemma. He understands that the end of the game looms.

On June 24, Crowhurst again finds a new option. His mind takes him on a fresh journey, one that has little to do with bankruptcy, sailing races, and an endless sea. At the top of a clean page in his logbook, he writes a title: "Philosophy." For the next week, he continues to write, producing twenty-five thousand words. He has Albert Einstein's book *Relativity: The Special and General Theory* with him, and he imagines a conversation with the famous physicist. Crowhurst writes, "I introduce this idea $\sqrt{-1}$ because [it] leads directly to the dark tunnel of the space-time continuum, and once technology emerges from this tunnel the 'world' will 'end' . . . in the sense that we will have access to the means of 'extra-physical' existence, making the need for physical existence superfluous."

There is a theme to Crowhurst's ramblings: that a person of great intelligence can alter and deliver himself from the usual restrictions and rules of the physical world. On July 1, he sets out to do exactly that. His final logbook entry reads: "I will play this game when I choose I will resign the game 11 20 40 There is no reason for harmful"

Ten days later, a British mail vessel pulls alongside the drifting *Teignmouth Electron* and finds neatly stacked logbooks, navigation plotting sheets, and a sink filled with dirty dishes.

There is no one aboard.

Would You? Could You?

(Share your answers if you're reading in a group)

In his book *The Ulysses Factor*, J. R. L. Anderson describes our admiration for the lone hero, a figure compelled to endure long and dangerous trials of exploration. We each have this genetic instinct, Anderson says—a combination of imagination, self-discipline, selfishness, endurance, fear, courage, and social instability—yet it's dormant in all but a few.

There is another viewpoint, which is that God imbues each of us with a need to stretch our abilities and deepen our faith, and that we find him in a way most real and vibrant when we are in the crucible of that testing. Some of us encounter him through the testing of relationships, careers, and service. Others discover him through the challenge of extreme adventure. As they scale the mountain or attack the seas, many are not even aware that this is what they seek.

Assessing motivation is a tricky business. Few of the participants in the 1968 Golden Globe race even tried to explain their reasons for setting out. Yet it's interesting to note the comments of Robin Knox-Johnston, who was not only the lone sailor to finish, but also, with the possible exception of Bernard Moitessier, the one who most enjoyed being alone at sea: "Throughout the voyage I never really felt I was completely alone, and I think a man would have to be inhumanly confident and self-reliant if he were to make this sort of voyage without faith in God."

What sort of man or woman are you—a product of the Ulysses factor, dependent on God, or something else entirely?

- Assuming you had the technical skill, *could you* handle a round-the-world sailing voyage—alone? *Would you* have taken on the challenge of the 1968 Golden Globe race?

- What role does faith in God play in taking on a long-term challenge? Do you agree or disagree with Robin Knox-Johnston's statement about inhuman confidence and self-reliance?
- The apostle Paul wrote, "We know that suffering produces perseverance; perseverance, character; and character, hope" (Rom. 5:3–4). Does extreme adventure require or produce perseverance—or both? Paul seems to say that suffering eventually leads to hope, but hope in what?
- What is it about a lengthy test that makes us consider giving in to temptation? What temptations did the Golden Globe racers face? How might being alone have multiplied those temptations?
- Clare Crowhurst, widow of Donald Crowhurst, recently said of her husband, "The man who went to sea would never have thought of cheating. But who knows what somebody goes through when they can't reach out and touch someone and receive human warmth?" What's your opinion of Donald Crowhurst—was he a conniving cheat? A tragic figure? A fool? Was he at all responsible for the apparent suicide of Nigel Tetley? If you were in Crowhurst's shoes, alone in the Atlantic in mid-November 1968, what would you have done?
- When it comes to temptation, what are your strong points? Where are you weakest?
- Scripture says, "God is faithful; he will not let you be tempted beyond what you can bear. But when you are tempted, he will also provide a way out so that you can stand up under it" (1 Cor. 10:13). Do you believe this? How can anyone resist temptation for months at a time?

Reporting In

Are you willing to suffer in order to acquire perseverance, character, and hope? Pray about it. Are you struggling with temptation in any area of your life? Pray about that too.

Hitting the Trail

(This is just for you)

If you haven't endured any long ocean voyages lately, it may be time to ratchet up your suffering and perseverance quotient—not because you're a sadomasochist, but because it can lead to character, hope, and a deeper faith. Let's get into it.

- Write down what "extreme adventure" means to you. It might be a twenty-mile hike, a fifty-mile bike ride, a glider flight, a canoe trip, a motorcycle tour, a summit attempt—or, if your mind and body are more accustomed to licorice and late nights with Letterman, maybe it's a jog around the park. Choose whatever it is that sounds exciting and will stretch you, and write down a plan here for making it happen.

  _____

  _____

  _____

  _____

- Make a list of goals for your adventure. Whether it's deepening your relationship, taking time for praise and worship, or simply admiring creation, be sure to include God in your reckoning.

  _____

  _____

  _____

  _____

- Do you know someone who has developed a strong ability to persevere? For that matter, who in your circle appears to easily handle temptation? Corner these people and ask them about their secrets.

_____

_____

_____

New Territory

(For those who want to explore further)
Read *A Voyage for Madmen*, Peter Nichols's bestselling account of the 1968 Golden Globe race, and watch the documentary *Deep Water*, an exploration of the saga of Donald Crowhurst.

- Of the nine participants in the round-the-world contest, whom do you admire the most? The least? Why? Which one most reminds you of you?
- Has your opinion of Donald Crowhurst changed? Why or why not?

7

The Open Road

Rise and go; your faith has made you well.

Luke 17:19

The morning air is crisp and cold, and a mist covers the valley floor as a man on a handcycle turns the crank that propels him down Highway 135 toward the town of Gunnison, Colorado. He's at the beginning of a rugged, 110-mile day's journey on the 2005 Bicycle Tour of Colorado, a weeklong ride through the Rocky Mountains.

For the man on the handcycle, forty-six-year-old Drew Wills, the tour is more than a casual outing. It's a test, a chance to find out if he's ready to resume his life after the horrific event that occurred exactly six months before.

Drew pushes on. He's already feeling the strain in his arms. Earlier in the week, brutal weather and fatigue twice forced him to drop out ahead of the finish line. He doesn't believe he's going to make it today either. He doesn't allow himself to think about the disappointment he'll feel if he again can't meet the challenge.

Are his days as a road warrior at an end?

Drew Wills is not a man who likes to sit still. An avid out-doorsman, his idea of a relaxing winter vacation away from his work as an attorney is strapping on skis and attacking the most challenging slopes he can find. That's why he and his family were at Aspen Highlands Ski Resort on the second-to-last day of 2004. It was supposed to be a routine outing on the slopes. But when humans and steep alpine skiing are involved, the potential for disaster is always just below the surface, like a jagged rock hidden beneath a blanket of snow.

For the Wills family, it was the end of a five-day vacation with Drew's brother Lawson. They'd been blessed with brilliant sunshine, fresh powder, and great runs down some of the area's premier slopes. Drew and his daughter, Krista, had been skiing together since the lifts opened. By late afternoon Krista's feet were frozen. When Drew's wife, Jeanie, found them in the lift line, she and Krista decided to head inside to warm up.

Drew wasn't ready to quit. He wanted to catch up with his brother and son, Stephen. "Why don't you two go on ahead?" Drew said. "I'll stay out a little longer and find the rest of 'em."

Drew rode the lift to the top of Steeplechase, a challenging but familiar run that featured large moguls. He took in the spectacular view along with a deep breath of crisp mountain air. Drew loved nearly any outdoor sport, especially mountain and road cycling, hiking, climbing, and of course, alpine skiing. He'd been on the slopes since he was four, when his dad began taking him and his brothers to the Monarch Ski Area from their home in Pueblo.

At the top, Drew pushed off with his poles to start his run. He was in his element—the breeze and the warmth of the sun on his face, the excitement of negotiating a steep slope made smooth and forgiving by more than a foot of fresh champagne powder, the effortless cadence of his skis turning, the simple joy of being in God's creation.

Everything was routine and under control when Drew slipped out of the chute that connected to Garmisch, another run. Suddenly, he tensed. Less than twenty feet away, a woman in a blue and black ski outfit, apparently uncomfortable with the terrain, was rapidly traversing sideways across the slope.

She was skiing directly into Drew's path.

Drew quickly took into account the woman's direction and maneuvered to avoid her. His attention was drawn from the rest of the slope for only a moment, but it was long enough to distract him from the pine with the foot-and-a-half-wide trunk that stood apart from the rest of the tree line. An instant later, Drew spotted the pine and tried to cut his turn even harder.

It was too late. The impact of Drew's lower body slamming into the tree launched him into the air. He spun in a complete circle and came to a stop.

Drew lay in the snow and tried to gather his senses. The pain in his lower back was intense, but otherwise he seemed okay. Then he looked down at his legs. His brain told him they were together, stretched out straight in front of him. His eyes, however, showed they were splayed out at strange angles to the side.

That's when Drew knew something was terribly wrong.

The accident had broken Drew's back and severed his spinal cord. He'd suffered what was later termed a complete T12 (twelfth thoracic vertebra) spinal cord injury.

He was paralyzed from the waist down.

For Drew, it was the beginning of a difficult journey to a new way of life. After evacuation off the mountain and a helicopter ride to a Grand Junction hospital, a surgeon inserted screws and two titanium rods to fuse his back. Ten days later he was flown to Englewood's Craig Hospital, a leading rehabilitation center.

Drew's first days at Craig included more than a few dark moments. Active and independent all his life, he was suddenly bedridden and receiving twenty-four-hour care. He had to adjust to the idea of being dependent on others. He was in considerable pain and filled with a variety of medications. He couldn't sleep—the nurses turned him every two hours, and his roommate kept a TV blaring day and night.

Then he got sick. He was vomiting and had a fever, severe headache, and full body rash. He'd never felt so awful. The doctors had theories but were unable to diagnose the problem.

Drew was already a man of faith. Almost from the moment of his accident, he had prayed. Now his petitions were more urgent than ever.

"Lord, I'm not sure what I'm going to do here," he prayed. "Please take away the pain. Please help the doctors discover what's wrong so I can get healthy and learn to function again. Please don't leave me like this. You're all I've got."

After a few days of misery, the doctors finally diagnosed Drew's illness—a urinary tract infection, relatively common for people with spinal cord injuries, combined with a reaction to the medication. As the proper medication took effect and Drew's infection and rash receded, his spirits rose. They jumped higher when Stephen showed him photos of handcycles and other adaptive outdoor equipment.

"Dad, you're going to have to do things in a different way, but you don't have to give anything up," Stephen said.

With the challenge of physical therapy ahead of him, Drew was determined to enhance what he could still do rather than dwell on what he'd lost. Though there were hard days, Drew knew he could count on the support of his wife, family, and friends. He also relied on his faith.

"You maintain hope by having trust in something that's bigger and greater than yourself," he said. "If you don't have that or lose it, you end up in despair. That's the alternative. It's pretty black-and-white."

Drew's days began at 8 a.m. with physical and occupational therapy sessions, Jeanie always by his side to encourage and support him. The first tasks were training his body to manage his blood pressure without the aid of his legs and learning to maintain balance in a sitting position. When Drew was on the edge of his bed, he felt as if he was on the edge of a cliff. He soon progressed to a "slider board," the method for getting from the bed to a wheelchair. Then there were physical and occupational therapy sessions in the rehab gym on mats, or what the patients call "slabs," as well as instruction on operating a wheelchair. Afternoons were filled with sessions such as recreational therapy, pool therapy, patient education classes, weight training, and learning to drive a car with hand controls.

There was no coddling of patients. If someone missed the beginning of a session, a staff member was sent to hunt the patient down. If there were repeated issues, the patient was discharged.

For Drew, the strict regimen and physical demands were welcome. He had to learn new ways to accomplish what used to be simple tasks, but the therapy and training were vital if he was to continue his active lifestyle. And staying active meant everything to Drew.

He was still at Craig when he sat down for the first time in a handcycle, the low-to-the-ground, three-wheeled vehicle powered by arm strength. He found it nearly impossible to get into and much slower than bicycling, but he realized it still took him where he wanted to go. His passion for cycling didn't have to end. The open road still beckoned.

Drew's recovery was slowed by additional urinary tract infections and a bone disorder complication. He struggled to wean himself off of the many medications used by the hospital to manage his pain and complications of his paralysis. Yet a little more than four months after the accident, Drew completed his rehabilitation and was discharged. He returned to his Colorado Springs home and almost didn't recognize it. Family, friends, and neighbors had remodeled it for a wheelchair-bound resident. Some of the same friends presented him with two new handcycles.

The outpouring of support from family and so many others brought tears to Drew's eyes. He was overwhelmed and humbled that they believed in him. His family, his friends, and the community had given him the chance to again support his family, to continue to enjoy the activities he loved, and to once again be independent and productive. It allowed him to rebuild his confidence and, most importantly, dedicate himself to getting back on the road to a full and rewarding life.

Drew's family and Claire Cahow, his recreational therapist at Craig, encouraged him to put his handcycling skills to the test. The Wills family joined Adaptive Adventures, a group that promotes sports and recreation for people with physical disabilities, on the 2005 Bicycle Tour of Colorado.

Drew was uncertain if he'd be able to handle the rigors of caring for himself outside his home and riding each day on the tour. He knew it would include cycling up to a hundred miles a day through mountain passes that reached as high as twelve thousand feet. It would be a challenge unlike any he'd faced.

On the road toward Gunnison, the wind begins to blow. Drew's team—Jeanie, Stephen, Krista, and Claire Cahow—takes turns riding bicycles in front of Drew, reducing wind resistance for him. They also trade off driving their support vehicle, the family Land Cruiser.

They reach Gunnison in less than two hours but still have more than eighty miles to go. Drew pushes on past the Blue Mesa Reservoir and into the green pine forest and mountainous terrain of Black Canyon. As the temperature climbs toward the nineties, he can feel the sweat on his back and the ache in his arms, but he keeps turning the crank that keeps his wheels moving. Drew is exhausted, but he's not giving up yet.

At the end of the long downhill stretch that marks the end of Black Canyon, the landscape changes dramatically. Drew and his team enter a valley that opens into the scrub oak and grassy fields of the desert and plains. Drew's outlook begins to change too. He thinks, *You know, I just might be able to do this.*

The feeling grows, nurtured by encouraging shouts from Jeanie and Claire on their bikes ahead of Drew. "You're doing awesome!" they say. "This is incredible!"

They are nearing the century mileage mark, fifteen miles from the finish at Hotchkiss, when the feeling blossoms into certainty. "You're gonna do it, Drew," Jeanie calls back. She and Claire exchange glances. Both see that the other's eyes are welling with tears.

He's going to make it, Jeanie thinks. *We've put it all in God's hands, and everything's going to be okay. He's back.*

Drew is thinking beyond the finish line at Hotchkiss. *If I can do this, there are all kinds of things I can do.* Suddenly, despite the hardship of the last months, the future looks unlimited.

The Tour of Colorado is only the beginning. In 2007 Drew places second at the Off-Road Handcycling World Championships at Crested Butte, Colorado, and in 2009 he wins the event. Also in 2009, competing against some of the world's best international racers, he is the second American finisher among long-seat riders in the Sadler's Alaska Challenge, the longest and toughest handcycle race on the planet. He returns to full-time work as an attorney, trying cases in the courtroom, serving on local nonprofit boards, and providing for his family. He also regains his enjoyment of Colorado's slopes on a monoski and celebrates his twenty-fifth wedding anniversary by earning open water certification and scuba diving with his wife in the Caribbean.

Drew may be sitting down more, but he's not slowing down. The open road still beckons.

Would You? Could You?

(Share your answers if you're reading in a group)

There is a Bible verse that says, "God causes all things to work together for good to those who love God, to those who are called according to His purpose" (Rom. 8:28 NASB). If you're lying in the snow with a broken back and paralyzed limbs—or listening to your spouse tell you they want a divorce—or receiving a phone call that your child has been killed in an accident—that idea can be more than a little hard to accept. Where's the good in any of those?

Jim Daly, president of Focus on the Family, says part of the good is that when God allows us to be broken, either emotionally, spiritually, or physically, it encourages us to move deeper into a relationship with him. "I'm convinced," Daly says, "that even though the Lord chooses not to exercise control over our attitudes and faith, he is continually arranging circumstances that give us the opportunity to choose the broken path to him."

Drew Wills, at least, seems to have responded that way after his accident. "When you wake up every day with a reminder that certain unexpected events in life may leave you helpless and alone, even if you work hard and learn to overcome them, it's easier to depend on God," he says. "It's a constant reminder that he is your salvation and you have a lot to be thankful for."

The next time you're on the wrong end of devastating news or tragedy, how will you respond?

- *Could you*, like Drew Wills, be thankful for *anything* after an injury that leaves you paralyzed? *Would you* persevere through rehabilitation to make the most of your new life, or would you descend into anger, bitterness, and despair?
- Do you believe God causes the bad things that happen to us, either sometimes or all of the time? Or does he allow them to happen and then step in to work things for good if we love and seek him? Or is the bad stuff simply happenstance?
- In what ways can we gain from enduring hardship and suffering?
- If you are a parent, do you ever cause or allow bad things to happen to your children (think discipline)?

What are the benefits of discipline for a child? Do the same concepts apply between us and God?

- C. S. Lewis wrote, "God whispers to us in our pleasures, speaks in our conscience, but shouts in our pain: it is His megaphone to rouse a deaf world." Do you agree that the Lord uses pain to get our attention? Has he ever used pain to rouse you?
- Read Jeremiah 18:2–6. Can God mold us more easily for his purposes when things are sailing along smoothly or when our lives are falling apart and we feel broken?
- Drew Wills says family and friends played an enormous role in his recovery. The same guys he'd cycled and skied with rallied around him after his accident. How important is the support and fellowship of family and friends in persevering through a trial? Whom do you count on most when facing a difficult struggle? Who can count on you?

Reporting In

Do you allow your circumstances to define God or do you allow God to define your circumstances? Take up the matter with the Lord.

Hitting the Trail

(This is just for you)

My (Peb's) wife, Sharon, is a former rehabilitation liaison nurse. She says you can tell how a person will adjust to a disabling injury by his or her attitude toward life *before* it happens. I was in the hospital with Drew Wills on the day of his accident. I knew my friend's faith, character, and practice, and I understood that despite this horrific injury, he would find a way to overcome the challenge and excel at this new stage in his journey.

So much of our ability to endure and persevere through hard times depends on our attitude. The apostle Paul wrote, "Be joyful always; pray continually; give thanks in all circumstances, for this is God's will for you in Christ Jesus" (1 Thess. 5:16–18). But when you're dealing with a debilitating injury or illness or the death of someone close, how do you find joy or gratitude?

- Write down here some of the things that bring you joy. Is there a difference between feeling happy and abiding in a soul-deep joy? What is the source of that kind of joy?

  _____

  _____

  _____

- List the people and things you are most thankful for today. How many items on your list would change if you, like Drew Wills, suddenly lost the use of your legs? Would you blame others or God for your condition? Would it change what you're thankful for?

  _____

  _____

  _____

- Paul also wrote, "I have learned the secret of being content in any and every situation . . . I can do everything through him who gives me strength" (Phil. 4:12–13). Record here what you believe is Paul's secret. Do you have this strength?

  _____

  _____

  _____

New Territory

(For those who want to explore further)
Read *Joni*, the autobiography of Joni Eareckson Tada, the woman who dove into Chesapeake Bay, struck a rock, and found herself paralyzed from the neck down.

- Are there any similarities between your faith journey and Joni's?
- What does it mean to surrender your life to the Lord?

8

To the Last Breath

You threw me into ocean's depths, into a watery grave,
with ocean waves, ocean breakers crashing over me.

Jonah 2:3 Message

John Chatterton is a diver. To earn a living, the forty-year-old with the Long Island accent works at underwater construction jobs in the Manhattan area. But his passion is shipwreck diving—the deeper and more daring, the better.

Many wreck divers are in the game only for "tonnage"—to fill their mesh goody bags with as many dishes, gear, and artifacts from a dead ship as they can. Chatterton has removed his share too, but for him it's about more than hauling up stuff. Diving is about exploration, about mapping the unknown. It's a chance to see what no one else has seen.

By the fall of 1991, few wrecks on America's eastern seaboard remain unexplored. So when a fishing boat captain gives Chatterton's mentor, diving legend Bill Nagle, the latitude and longitude of a site sixty miles off the New Jersey coast that promises to be "something big," Chatterton is quick to sign up for the dive. It's probably just a garbage barge or even a pile of rocks. But Chatterton has to find out.

On September 2, Nagle and thirteen men reach the mystery site aboard Nagle's dive boat, the *Seeker*. He and Chatterton examine the boat's electronic bottom finder. Something is there, but it's deeper than the men expected, about 230 feet below the surface. This is dangerous territory. No one has much experience at 230 feet.

Shipwreck divers face many risks. A broken pipe can cut an air hose. Loose cables can tangle up with oxygen tanks. And then there is nitrogen narcosis, every undersea explorer's nightmare. At depths greater than sixty-six feet, a diver's judgment and motor skills begin to falter. At more than one hundred feet below, the deterioration can be significant. Many a diver, confused by narcosis, has lost his way inside the twisting labyrinth that is the guts of a shipwreck. And the diver who stays too long cannot simply shoot for the surface. He must rise gradually, allowing the nitrogen he's accumulated from breathing gas to release into his bloodstream in tiny bubbles. If he surfaces too quickly, he risks the "bends"—large bubbles that form outside the bloodstream and block circulation. The result can be agonizing pain, paralysis, and death.

That's why, on the *Seeker*, the decision is that Chatterton will dive first, alone, to see if anything down there is worth the risk.

Chatterton splashes over the side. Six minutes later he lands on something hard. Even with his headlight, he can't see much at this depth—the water is a murky green and a snowstorm of white matter moves sideways around him. But he can make out patches of rust on metal and, above him, a curved railing and corner. He thinks it's a strange shape for what's probably a barge.

Chatterton moves slowly along the top of the wreck, careful to keep hold of it so the current doesn't carry him away. He comes to an open hatch and pokes his head and headlight inside.

It's a room. His light illuminates an object lying against one of the walls. The object is shaped like a cigar. It has fins and a propeller.

It isn't possible. Chatterton closes his eyes and opens them again.

The object is unmistakable. It's a torpedo.

I'm narced, Chatterton thinks. *I'm at 220 feet. I'm exhausted from fighting the current. I could be seeing things.*

You are on top of a submarine, another voice inside his brain replies.

There are no submarines anywhere near this part of the ocean. I have books. I have studied books. There are no submarines here. This is impossible.

You are on top of a submarine.

I'm narced.

There is no other shape like that torpedo. Remember those rolled edges you saw on the hull, the ones that looked built for gliding? Submarine. You have just discovered a submarine.

This is a huge dive.

No, John, this is more than a huge dive. This is the holy grail.

Chatterton recognizes from the deterioration of metal around him that the submarine must have sunk about a half-century ago. That places it during World War II. He also knows there are no sunken American submarines in the vicinity.

"I'm holding on to a U-boat," Chatterton says aloud. "I'm holding on to a World War II German U-boat."

As incredible as this realization is, finding the submarine isn't nearly as important to Chatterton as identifying it. It is part of his personal code, one he'd begun to develop as a boy, modeled in part by his grandfather. Rae Emmet Arison was a retired rear admiral who'd commanded submarines in the 1930s and led battleships in World War II. He was also a man who valued excellence and persistence.

Chatterton's code crystallized further during his service as a medic in the Vietnam War. He became known as a different

101

kind of medic, one who risked everything to retrieve wounded and exposed soldiers, one who volunteered for patrols and often walked point. His experiences led him to identify a series of principles on the right way and wrong way to live.

The right way to live after discovering a U-boat is to identify it. For Chatterton, anything less is unacceptable.

That day in the ocean off the New Jersey coast becomes a defining moment in Chatterton's life. It is the beginning of a personal voyage to discovery and danger.

Some will call it a deadly obsession.

Two weeks after finding the submarine, almost all of the original thirteen divers return to the U-boat site. One is Steve Feldman, a stagehand at CBS television. Feldman and a buddy, excavation contractor Paul Skibinski, make their first dive of the day and penetrate a gaping hole in the sub's control room.

According to their conservative diving plan, after thirteen minutes inside, it's already time to go. Skibinski taps Feldman on the shoulder and points up. Feldman nods his okay. Skibinski turns and swims to the anchor line attached to the *Seeker*.

Skibinski looks behind him. Feldman has his back to Skibinski and seems to be checking out something on the wreck. Skibinski looks closer. No bubbles are rising from Feldman's regulator.

Something's not right, Skibinski thinks.

He swims over and turns his friend around.

Feldman's regulator falls from his mouth. He isn't blinking. He isn't breathing. He's gone.

Later, the divers speculate that Feldman simply blacked out, a not-uncommon occurrence at such depths.

Despite the tragedy, Chatterton, Nagle, and others—including dive-shop manager John Yurga and a new Chatterton ally, diver Richie Kohler—continue their quest to identify the sub. Chatterton flies to Chicago to study a U-boat at a museum. He communicates with U-boat experts in the United States and Germany. He pores over history books. Chatterton, Yurga, and Kohler make trips to the Naval Historical Center and the National Archives and Records Administration in Washington, D.C. Chatterton and Yurga fly to Germany to investigate more possibilities.

As they research, one U-boat after another surfaces as the likely candidate to solve the puzzle. And as they dig deeper, each theory is shot down by new evidence. The mystery of what they start calling the "U-Who" deepens.

In October 1992, the men are back on the ocean in the *Seeker*, still searching for answers. This time the team includes Chris and Chrissy Rouse, a father-son tandem famous for their cave diving exploits.

On the first day, in the forward torpedo room, Chatterton snags a piece of aluminum. On deck, he discovers it's a schematic of a section of the U-boat. Inscribed along the edge are the words "Bauart IXC" and "Deschimag, Bremen." It's a revealing find—IXC is a type of U-boat and Deschimag, Bremen is a German shipyard. The information will narrow their search significantly.

On the second day of the trip, the weather turns nasty and promises to get worse. Only six of the fourteen divers decide to hit the water. Two of the six are the Rouses.

On a previous dive, Chrissy had found a piece of canvas with German writing on it in the galley, wedged under a tall steel cabinet. This time he returns to the galley, determined to free the canvas and discover its secrets. His father remains outside the wreck and shines a light for Chrissy to find on his return. The Rouses have twenty minutes.

For roughly fifteen minutes, Chrissy digs under the cabinet, sending silt everywhere. The canvas loosens, but not enough for it to be removed. Chrissy pulls with greater force. The canvas begins to come free—and so does the steel cabinet. It topples onto Chrissy, pinning him. He's trapped.

Outside the wreck, Chris Rouse can't see anything through the thick cloud of silt. But their time is up, and Chrissy is still in there. He swims into the galley, finds his son beneath the cabinet, and works to free him. Ten minutes later, both

Rouses swim out of the galley. But the nylon line Chrissy extended into the galley is tangled from his struggle to escape. Narcosis further warps their judgment.

For their decompression, the Rouses had placed oxygen tanks forty feet aft of their entry point in the sub, near the anchor line to the *Seeker*. But now, disoriented and panicked, they swim in the wrong direction. The tanks are nowhere to be found. After forty minutes underwater and with little air left, both do the unthinkable—they forego decompression and shoot to the surface.

It is a fatal move. The bends kill Chris Rouse on board the *Seeker*. A Coast Guard helicopter rushes Chrissy to a New York hospital, where he dies a few hours later.

It's a devastating loss, but Chatterton won't stop now. One of his principles is that "the worst possible decision is to give up." He, along with Kohler and others, continues to research. The price of their quest grows ever higher. Late in 1993, Bill Nagle drinks himself to death. Both Chatterton's and Kohler's marriages collapse.

More theories on the identity of the sub are embraced and quashed. Then, in early 1994, comes a breakthrough. A British U-boat expert discovers that *U-869*, a German submarine believed to have been sunk off Gibraltar, may have never received its orders to proceed to the coast of North Africa. It may have continued on its original mission—to patrol American shores southeast of New York.

Further Chatterton research shows that the classification of *U-869*'s sinking off Gibraltar is shaky at best. But for Chatterton, a strong theory isn't enough. He has to know for certain.

Three more years of inconsequential dives and frustration pass. Chatterton and the rest have explored every room on the sub except one—the electric motor room. The problem is that the room is blocked by a heavy oil tank that's fallen in the diesel motor room. There's an opening just below the ceiling, but it's too small for a diver with oxygen tanks to wriggle through.

On August 31, 1997—almost six years to the day after finding the U-boat—Chatterton implements the final stage of a daring plan and swims into the diesel motor room. He's wearing one oxygen tank instead of two. Chatterton removes his lone source of air, pushes it and a sledgehammer through the opening that leads to the electric motor room, then slips through himself. He reattaches the oxygen tank.

The week before, Chatterton had entered the electric motor room the same way and videotaped a stack of boxes. He believes they are filled with spare parts that include tags that will conclusively identify the wreck. But the boxes are held in place by a heavy, five-foot section of pipe.

Chatterton swims deeper into the electric motor room and finds the boxes and pipe. He swings the sledgehammer, stirring up a cloud of rust particles. When the particles settle, Chatterton is dismayed. The pipe hasn't moved. And it's not a pipe at all. With the rust gone, he can see it's actually a pressurized oxygen tank. The sledgehammer blow could easily have triggered an explosion and killed him.

He has a decision to make.

When things are easy, a person doesn't really learn about himself, Chatterton thinks. *It's what a person does at the moment of his greatest struggle that shows him who he really is. Some people never get that moment.*

The U-Who is my moment. What I do now is what I am.

Chatterton lifts the sledgehammer and smashes it against the tank. Rust and silt again swirl about him, but there's no explosion—just the sound of metal against metal.

The cloud clears. The tank has fallen away.

Chatterton slips the smallest box, a bit bigger than a shoe box, into his mesh bag and swims out to the tiny opening in the diesel room. He pushes the box through to Kohler, who's accompanied him on the dive. Kohler passes it on to another diver who will send the box to the surface.

But Chatterton isn't finished. He's still got three minutes, time for another box.

The next box is bigger and heavier. Chatterton starts rolling it out. He realizes it's taking too much time. He's got to go.

Chatterton's efforts have stirred up the silt again. He's got no visibility. He swims up to navigate his way out along the ceiling. He's only a few feet away from the opening to freedom when something pulls him back by the neck. It's a wire hanging from the ceiling, looped around him.

He tries moving backward slowly. It makes things worse—the gear on his back also becomes entangled with cables.

Chatterton no longer has time to be careful. He rips the wire away from his throat. He struggles against the other cables once, then again. He's still trapped. He puts all his strength into the effort.

He's free. His oxygen tank is also down to its last breath of air.

Chatterton swims through the narrow opening near the ceiling, discards his oxygen tank, and pushes hard for his decompression oxygen bottles, located on top of the sub, forty feet away. He feels his lungs on the verge of bursting. It's going to be close.

Seconds later Chatterton finds the bottles, stuffs a regulator into his mouth, and turns a valve. He can breathe again. He's made it.

For nearly two hours, Chatterton silently decompresses with Kohler as they gradually move closer to the surface. The decompression is almost over when a diver swims down and hands Chatterton a slate with words written on it. They read:

The U-Who now has a name—it is *U-869*. Congratulations.

Would You? Could You?

(Share your answers if you're reading in a group)

Webster's dictionary defines *obsession* as "a persistent disturbing preoccupation with an often unreasonable idea or feeling." The lore of the sea is filled with examples of such compulsion, perhaps best illustrated by the fictional Captain Ahab in Melville's *Moby-Dick*. Like Ahab, John Chatterton was on a quest and would not be deterred. His motivation, however, was based more on a philosophy of life than on revenge.

Whether we recognize it or not, most of us are guided by a set of core beliefs that help direct our daily actions and decisions. Part of the adventure of living is discovering and embracing what we believe. Chatterton's beliefs on the right way to live led him to pursue the identification of the U-Who with single-minded intensity. He once told his wife, "I'm being tested. What I do with this U-boat is what I am as a person." Chatterton succeeded in the end, but he and others also paid dearly for the triumph.

How about it—do you have a "right way" to live? And how far are you willing to go to uphold your beliefs?

- If you were a skilled deep-sea diver and you'd found a mystery U-boat, *would you* feel compelled to identify it? *Could you* persevere when the going got tough?
- Do you respect John Chatterton for his efforts to identify *U-869* or do you think he was out of his mind—or both? Why?
- Is there ever a limit to how far a person should go in doing the right thing? Where is that line?
- Do you think Chatterton was being tested by his encounter with the U-boat? If so, did he pass the test?
- Do you agree with Chatterton's statement that what you do at the moment of your greatest struggle shows who you truly are?
- How important are excellence and persistence to your core beliefs?
- What should a person base his or her beliefs on: Experience? Logic? Faith? Why?

- The Bible says, "Love the LORD your God and keep his requirements, his decrees, his laws and his commands always" (Deut. 11:1). Is this our guide to the right way to live? Why or why not?

Reporting In

Are you facing any tests of your commitment to excellence and perseverance today? If so, ask the Lord to show you how he wants you to handle them.

Hitting the Trail

(This is just for you)

John Chatterton's principles on life include statements like these: "If you follow in another's footsteps, you miss the problems really worth solving"; "Excellence is born of preparation, dedication, focus, and tenacity"; "It is easiest to live with a decision if it is based on an earnest sense of right and wrong."

Few of us take the trouble to write down the principles that we strive to live by. Now is your chance.

- Record here the central beliefs and principles that comprise the person you are (or wish to be). Take your time.

_____

_____

_____

- Go through each item on your list. How are you illustrating (or failing to illustrate) each principle? List examples.

_____

_____

_____

- What are the principles that Jesus Christ appeared to live by on earth? How do his principles compare with yours? What does this mean to you?

  _____

  _____

  _____

New Territory

(For those who want to explore further)

Read *Shadow Divers*, Robert Kurson's bestselling tale of the quest to identify *U-869*, and watch *Hitler's Lost Sub*, the public television documentary about the same.

- How did Richie Kohler's "right way to live" differ from John Chatterton's? Did Kohler pass his own test?
- How would you have fared as a sailor on a German U-boat?

PART THREE

COURAGE

9

Fear and Friendship at the Top of the World

The LORD will watch over your coming and
going both now and forevermore.

Psalm 121:8

Eric Alexander pauses on a near-vertical slope to kick
ice off his crampons and gulp another mouthful of
oxygen-depleted air. He's thrilled to be here—twenty-
two thousand feet above sea level, ascending the western flank
of Lhotse that leads to the peak of Mount Everest. But he's
also concerned. The Lhotse face is difficult under any circumstances, but this season, as the ice and snow melt, it's
raining down a frightening amount of debris.

And Eric has more than his own neck to worry about. The
thirty-two-year-old is part of a team that hopes to guide his
friend and fellow climber, Erik Weihenmayer, to Everest's
summit. Weihenmayer is attempting to become the first blind
person to reach the top of the world.

Eric has led his friend most of the morning. He has a bell attached to his pack so Weihenmayer can follow the sound, and he calls out instructions such as "Deep crevasse here—you gotta jump all the way across" and "Chunky ice here—you need to raise your right leg high." Now, however, he's about two hundred feet above Weihenmayer and his teammates.

Suddenly, something dark, about the size of a softball, hurtles past Eric.

"Rock!" he yells, a warning to those below. To his horror, he sees the missile is headed straight for Weihenmayer.

Even if he could see it coming, Weihenmayer would have no time to dodge. He freezes. The rock slams into the snow at his feet and bounces down the slope.

Whoa, that was close, Eric thinks. *Thank goodness it didn't hit him. Let's move!*

The team has nearly reached camp 3 at 23,500 feet when Eric stops to check his heart rate. After the stress of hauling a big load to camp 2 the day before, it was high all night. Now he finds it's still high: over 180 beats a minute. Reluctantly, Eric decides he's pushed himself too hard; he needs to reduce altitude. After a conversation with Weihenmayer, he turns around and begins retracing his path on the icy Lhotse face back to camp 2. Five minutes later, as he picks his way down an especially steep slope, he's satisfied he's made the hard but right decision.

His thoughts are interrupted by a strange thumping sound from above. He looks up. A boulder the size of a truck tire is hurtling straight at him. It's less than one hundred feet away.

Eric's reaction is instinctive. He tucks his head and makes two quick hops to his left.

Is it enough?

The boulder flies past, missing Eric by inches. If he'd stayed in position, he'd very likely be dead.

Eric draws one long, deep breath. Then he drops to one knee on the slope.

Lord, please keep me safe the rest of the way down.

He continues his descent at a much quicker pace.

The manager of a mountaineering shop in Vail, Colorado, and a devoted climber, Eric met Weihenmayer through his roommate in late 1997 and found they had similar interests in climbing. Soon they were joining forces on increasingly difficult ice climbs in Colorado. Weihenmayer's lack of vision barely slowed him down. Eric realized it was more inconvenience than obstacle.

On another climb with Weihenmayer, one question changed Eric's future. "I've got this idea to climb Everest," Weihenmayer said. "I'm putting some friends together, and I think you'd be a good addition to the team. What do you think?"

For Eric, it was the opportunity to achieve a lifelong dream, one he never expected to fulfill. There was just one qualification—a successful "practice run" on the 22,500-foot Ama Dablam, seven miles south of Everest.

That's how Eric found himself in the Himalayas in April 2000, pinned in a tent with Weihenmayer for six days, waiting for a storm to pass. The deteriorating weather finally forced the team to abandon its summit hopes.

Eric descended Ama Dablam with three teammates and two Sherpas. After enduring a long session of down climbing and rappels through freezing wind and snow, Eric was exhausted and ready to crawl into his sleeping bag in his tent at camp 1. With the tents in sight, he unclipped from the end of the fixed rope and started the short but still dangerous descent down the narrow, steep path to camp. Below the path was a nearly vertical drop of more than six hundred feet.

All it took was one wrong step. The three-foot rock beneath his boot began to slide. Eric's feet went out from under him. He fell on the rock and felt himself and the rock slipping. He grabbed for the edge of the path, but his heavy gloves found no traction.

He was going down.

He bounced off the slope and was airborne for a few feet, and then he slammed against the mountain again, his hel-

115

meted head cracking against rock, before being flung once more into space.

His thoughts distilled to single-word sentences: *Help! Stop!*

And then he wasn't falling. His feet slid against a protrusion on the mountain and held there. With his stomach against the face, Eric slowly turned his head and looked down.

He was amazed by what he saw. He was "standing" on a ledge about three feet long and extending two feet out of the slope. It was the only barrier on the face. Below it was another sheer drop of nearly five hundred feet.

Eric did a quick self-check. His elbow hurt and his climbing outfit was shredded, but he hadn't broken any bones. It was as if God had said, "No, Eric, not today."

His teammates lowered a rope, and Eric climbed back to camp. His ordeal wasn't over, however. That night, because of the shock of the fall, he developed high-altitude pulmonary edema. His lungs filled with fluid. His oxygen saturation rate—a normal level is 97 to 99 percent—dropped to 45 percent. The expedition doctor told Eric they needed to get him off the mountain quickly. He didn't mention that with that much fluid in his lungs, Eric should already be dead.

A snowstorm, the altitude, and the steep slope made a helicopter rescue impossible. Eric was forced to rappel from camp 1 and then walk with the doctor to base camp, where a helicopter flew him to a hospital.

It was a trying time. As he attempted to recover, Eric caught pneumonia. The Everest expedition was only eight months away. He found himself praying for signs that he should stay home.

Eric realized he was afraid.

There was justification for his fear. People who develop high-altitude pulmonary edema once are more likely to suffer from it again. Eric wondered if his teammates would see him as bad luck or someone who had to be watched. He didn't want to put his family through more trauma after they'd just recovered from his fall on Ama Dablam.

He also considered warnings emerging from the climbing community. Some felt that Weihenmayer was putting his life, as well as the lives of his teammates, at unwarranted risk. If Weihenmayer didn't reach the summit or if anything went wrong, people would see the expedition as a failure. Eric didn't want to let his friend down.

As Eric weighed his decision, he was rocked by a heart-breaking loss. His prayer partner, climbing buddy, and best friend, a free spirit named Joseph, went snowboarding alone into backcountry near Vail. When he didn't show up for work the next day, Eric and a team of ski patrol friends mounted a search. They found Joseph at the bottom of a cliff, upside down in the snow. He'd suffocated.

Eric knew Joseph wanted him to go to Everest. *I can't just quit*, he thought. *He'd be so mad at me if I did.*

A Boulder doctor cleared Eric to go. His teammates encouraged him to come back. The final hurdle was Weihenmayer himself. Eric asked what he thought he should do.

"People have always made judgments on what I can and can't do," Weihenmayer said. "I'm not about to do the same thing to you. You've got to decide for yourself."

As Eric thought about it, he realized that the Everest expedition was about more than his own struggle. It had the potential to open new horizons for the blind and anyone held back by what seemed an insurmountable obstacle. He wanted to be part of that. He also sensed the Lord's direction through Bible verses such as Joshua 1:9: "Be strong and courageous . . . for the LORD your God will be with you wherever you go."

"I'm not sure if I'm strong enough to get you to the top or get myself to the top," he told Weihenmayer a few days later, "but I know I'm strong enough to help you get there."

On Everest in March and April 2001, Eric has plenty of opportunities to wonder if he's made the right decision. Weihenmayer's first trip through the treacherous Himalayan glacier known as the Khumbu Icefall takes thirteen intense hours instead of the scheduled seven, putting the goal of a summit in serious doubt. Then there is the issue with Eric's heart rate, followed by the rock-dodging adventure on the Lhotse face.

But Weihenmayer and Eric both persevere. As the climbers acclimatize to the altitude, repeatedly moving up and down the mountain, Weihenmayer gradually improves his speed through the icefall to a much quicker five hours. Eric's health problems disappear, and he rejoins the rest of the team.

Finally, on May 24, after two years of preparation and weeks of climbing and waiting for the right weather on the mountain, Eric, Weihenmayer, and the rest of the team are at camp 4, ready for the summit push.

The mood is a combination of excitement, nervous anticipation, and bald fear. Even while sitting in a tent at twenty-six thousand feet, every breath is labored, and simple decisions require intense concentration. The climbers are in the Death Zone, a place where no human can expect to live for long. They're well aware that the day before, an Austrian climber clipped into the wrong rope at the Hillary Step and fell. It was a fatal mistake.

By radio, the team gets word that a Spanish climber is missing somewhere on the slopes above them. Some begin preparing to aid in the search. Eric is asked to pray. He does, silently, and encourages the others to do the same. Minutes later, the team receives the good news that the missing climber is found and everyone's okay.

At 9 p.m. that night, wearing a green down suit, backpack, oxygen tank, and goggles, Eric steps out of his tent onto the South Col. He's greeted by subzero temperatures and a punishing wind. Everest is in the jet stream, where the air can easily fly faster than one hundred miles per hour. It's time to move.

Every step is a struggle, but the climbers push forward. Eric is just behind Weihenmayer, focused on making sure his friend stays on route. When they reach the Southeast Ridge at 27,500 feet, they trudge into a storm marked by lightning and snow. It appears they'll have to turn around, until base camp radios a forecast: the storm will pass. Coated in two inches of snow, they decide to continue up.

At 8:30 in the morning, the climbers reach the South Summit, three hundred vertical feet from the peak but still two hours of climbing away. They must negotiate a knife-edge ridge more than six hundred feet long. On the left side is a seven-thousand-foot drop into Nepal. On the right is a ten-thousand-foot drop into Tibet.

Eric looks at the precarious ridge and shakes his head. *How are we going to get across this?* But Weihenmayer is already on his way. Eric isn't going to leave his friend now.

The weather is clearing when they attack the Hillary Step, the thirty-nine-foot rock face named after the first man to ascend the world's tallest peak. Eric is just behind Weihenmayer when his friend takes hold of a rope, one of several that stretch down from the top of the face. Some are new and secure; some have been here for multiple climbing seasons.

Eric remembers the fate of the Austrian. He tells Weihenmayer, "Hey, Erik, there are a bunch of ropes here. Don't grab just one. Grab 'em all."

Finally, far above the clouds and beneath a brilliant blue sky, Eric, Weihenmayer, and the rest of the team make the final steps up to the small platform that marks the roof of the world.

"Wooo!" Eric shouts.

"Erik, you did it, man! You showed 'em!" yells another teammate.

"I can't believe it," says Weihenmayer.

It's a joyful moment marked by backslaps and hugs. But Eric has one private duty to perform. He's been carrying a picture of Joseph against his chest throughout the summit push. Now he takes it out, intending to secure it under a rock at the summit.

The wind has other ideas. The photo is ripped from Eric's hands. It begins a flight into the seemingly endless airspace

119

over Tibet, the birth of a new adventure. Startled at first, Eric quickly realizes that his friend would probably prefer it this way.

The team doesn't linger—they know how unforgiving this mountain can be to those who underestimate its power. Eric attaches the bell to his pack and prepares to lead Weihenmayer back into the world of mortals. He pauses one last time to speak to the Source of even greater power.

Thank you, Lord, for Joseph's and Erik's friendship, and for allowing us to make it this far. Please help us to get down safely.

Feeling stronger than ever, Eric steps off the summit and toward his next challenge.

Would You? Could You?

(Share your answers if you're reading in a group)

Before the Weihenmayer expedition, many people questioned the idea of a blind man attempting to summit Everest. Climber and author Jon Krakauer wrote to Weihenmayer, "I am not at all enthusiastic about your trip to Everest next spring . . . I don't think you can get to the top of that particular hill without subjecting yourself to horrendous risk, the same horrendous risk all Everest climbers face, and then some." Ed Viesturs, one of America's most prolific climbers, said in an interview, "I support his going. But I wouldn't want to take him up there myself . . . They'll have to be helping him, watching out for him every step of the way." That skepticism continued on the mountain itself. One climber planned to stay close to the expedition so he could "get the first picture of the dead blind guy." Even at camp 4, just before the final summit push, another climber stuck his head into one of the team's tents and, without realizing Weihenmayer was there, said, "You're gonna have a heck of a time getting that blind guy up there."

Weihenmayer's team was far from typical, however. Eric and the others were more than just experienced climbers. They were friends who had climbed with Weihenmayer many times before. As Eric says, "We are the experts on ourselves, and as a team we trusted each other. We might let the mountain turn us back, but we weren't going to let the 'experts' stop us."

It takes fortitude and courage to push forward in the face of pessimism and doubt. How willing are you to take big risks when everyone around you says, "No way"?

- If you had the technical ability, *would you*, like Eric Alexander, accept an invitation to help a blind friend summit Everest? Why or why not? If you couldn't see, *would you* take on a challenge like Everest?

- Do you agree or disagree with Krakauer's comments— was the risk acceptable or too high? Why? Would your opinion be any different if someone on the expedition had been hurt or killed?

- Eric survived brushes with death on both Ama Dablam and Everest. He attributes the team's success and his survival to God's grace, saying, "There were too many close calls. How did nineteen of us (an Everest record for one expedition) make the summit? How did I come back without any strength or training?" Is Eric brave or foolhardy? How about Erik Weihenmayer? Do you think God was looking out for them?

- Read Psalm 121, which says, "The LORD will keep you from all harm" (v. 7). Sometimes bad things *do* happen to us, so what does this mean?

- How important was friendship and teamwork to this expedition? How important is it in your life?

- Eric teaches disabled skiers and works with an organization that educates and encourages youth with disabilities in the outdoors. What are you doing to help people overcome obstacles in their lives?

- Do you usually abide by the advice of the "experts" in your life? When have you gone against their counsel?

How did that turn out? What does it mean to be an "expert on yourself"?

Reporting In

Is anyone's "expert" opinion holding you back from pursuing God's calling on your life? Ask the Lord whether your expert's words are wise or misguided advice.

Hitting the Trail

(This is just for you)

Eric Alexander gives the credit for his courage on Everest to his standing with God. He knew he had a room reserved in heaven. "Ultimately, what made the climb possible for me was the knowledge that my soul was secure with him," Eric says. "I knew that if I died, that wouldn't be the worst thing that could happen to me. My teammates didn't have that security and confidence, and it showed."

It makes sense. It's easier to risk your life for a worthy cause if you're certain you're destined for a better, eternal life. So . . . how certain are you?

- Whether you've given your heart to Jesus Christ or not, write down what you believe would happen to your soul if you died today. What is the foundation for your belief? How sure are you—60 percent? Ninety percent? What would it take to make you absolutely certain?

  _____

  _____

  _____

- Maybe you're a believer, but your faith comes and goes. Read Matthew 14:29–31 and John 20:25. The faith of the disciples, who witnessed the physical presence of Jesus, wavered as well. Does this mean it's okay for us to doubt our faith? What causes you to doubt? How do you respond to 2 Corinthians 5:7?

_____

_____

_____

• What draws you closer to the presence of God? A sunrise? Time alone reading Scripture? A demanding climb on a dangerous mountain? Make a list of the environments and activities that lead you deeper in your faith journey. Write down how it might be possible for you to spend more time seeking the Lord and a certain faith.

_____

_____

_____

New Territory

(For those who want to explore further)

Watch *Farther Than the Eye Can See*, a documentary about the Weihenmayer team's Everest expedition directed by Michael Brown, and read *Touch the Top of the World*, Weihenmayer's biography through 2001.

• How willing are you to take on the responsibility for someone else's life, as Eric Alexander and the rest of his teammates did on Everest?
• At the end of his book, Weihenmayer says life would be easier if he could see, but he's not sure it would be more exciting or satisfying. How can risk and challenge make life more rewarding?

10

Death and Birth in Blue John Canyon

When we find inspiration, we need to take action
... even if it means making a hard choice or cutting out something and leaving it in your past.

Aron Ralston

Saturday, April 26, 2003, 2:51 p.m.
Blue John Canyon, Utah

Twenty-seven-year-old Aron Ralston stands in a slot canyon and weighs the dilemma before him. To continue down the canyon, he must go over a boulder the size of a bus tire that's wedged between the walls at his feet, then drop twelve feet to the canyon floor. Beyond the boulder, the walls rise sixty feet to the canyon rim and taper to just three feet wide. It's a narrow, open-roofed tunnel carved in stone.

Aron kicks at the boulder; it seems secure enough to hang from. He squats, puts his weight onto the boulder, turns to face the direction he just came from, and slides over the boulder so he's dangling, arms extended, from its front.

Unexpectedly, the boulder shifts.

Aron knows this is bad news. He lets go and drops to the rocks below.

He looks up. The boulder is falling on top of him. He throws his hands up to protect himself. The boulder bashes Aron's left hand against the south wall, then ricochets and smashes down on his right hand, ripping it down the wall for a foot before coming to rest between both walls, pinning Aron's right hand against the north wall.

The pain is excruciating. Aron pulls hard three times at his arm. He pushes with all his might on the boulder.

Nothing happens.

He's alone, hidden in a remote canyon in southeast Utah, and he's stuck.

---

6 p.m.

Aron scratches at the boulder, first with the file end and then with the knife blade of his multiuse tool. His progress is pitifully slow. The boulder has the same appearance as the dark material that formed the canyon lip. His blade is rapidly losing its sharpness. *This chock stone*, Aron thinks, *is the hardest thing here.*

Aron is an experienced outdoorsman. He's trained in search and rescue. He's just spent the winter climbing some of Colorado's highest and toughest peaks. He knows how to work out problems under pressure. He's a graduate of Carnegie Mellon, for heaven's sake. But none of his training and experiences has prepared him for what he faces now.

He'd planned only for a bike ride and day hike through the canyons. The bike is hidden far back on the trail behind some bushes. His resources now are a CD player, a video camera, a headlamp, a rock-climbing harness and rappelling gear, two

126

small burritos, and twenty-two ounces of water. Those and his brain are all he's got.

What makes matters worse is that Aron has committed a cardinal sin for outdoor adventurers. Because he wanted to keep his options open, he left no detailed description of his plans. The only hint he gave his roommates in Aspen, Colorado, was a single word: Utah.

Unless he finds a way to get out of here, he'll miss the party at his home on Monday night. He'll miss the first day he's due back at his job at Ute Mountaineering on Tuesday. Eventually, people will begin searching. But it will be too late. With so little water, Aron figures he'll last until Monday or Tuesday morning at best.

"You're gonna have to cut your arm off," Aron says out loud.

"But I don't wanna cut my arm off!" He's arguing with himself.

"Aron, you're gonna have to cut your arm off."

Yet he knows he can't saw through his arm bones with his small, dull knife.

He scratches at the boulder some more.

Sunday, 1 p.m.

With his climbing gear, Aron's rigged a pulley system around the boulder in an attempt to move it. But the system is too weak. No matter how hard he tries, the boulder won't budge. It must weigh two hundred pounds, maybe more.

Suddenly, Aron hears the echo of voices in the canyon.

Could it be? It's the right time of day—a group would get to this part and be able to return out to the West Fork or to Horseshoe Trailhead in daylight.

"Help!" he shouts. "Helllp!"

Aron's heart pounds, but there is no other sound. Then he hears the echo again. This time, Aron recognizes what it really is—a kangaroo rat scratching in its nest above the boulder.

With few other options, Aron again considers amputation. He can fashion a tourniquet from materials at hand. He wonders, assuming he figures out a way to cut through his bones, if he has the courage to go through with it.

Aron presses the knife blade of his multitool against his arm near the wrist. He can see tendons and veins beneath the skin. He feels nauseous.

What are you doing, Aron? Get that knife away from your wrist! What are you trying to do, kill yourself? That's suicide! I don't care how good a tourniquet you have, you've got too many arteries in your arm to stop them all. You'll bleed out.

The idea of slashing his wrists to end the ordeal flashes through Aron's mind.

"I . . . hate . . . this!"

Sunday evening

Aron rests his left hand on the boulder and closes his eyes.

"God, I am praying to you for guidance," he says. "I'm trapped here in Blue John Canyon—you probably know that—and I don't know what I am supposed to do. I've tried everything I can think of. I need some new ideas. Or if I need to try something again—lifting the boulder, amputating my arm—please show me a sign."

Aron waits. There's no discernible answer.

Monday, 3 p.m.

Aron pulls out his video camera. He's already recorded an explanation of the accident. Now it's time to leave more thoughts.

"One of the things I'm learning here is that I didn't enjoy the people's company that I was with enough, or as much as I should have," he says. "A lot of really good people have spent a lot of time with me. Very often I would tend to ignore or diminish their presence in seeking the essence of the experience. All that's to say, I'm figuring some things out . . .

"I'm doing what I can, but this sucks. It's really bad. This is one of the worst ways to go. Knowing what's going to happen, but it still being three or four days out."

He pauses.

"I did want to say, on the logistical side of things, I have some American Express insurance that should cover costs of the recovery operation when that does happen . . ."

Tuesday morning
Aron is recording again.

"This next part may not be for all viewers at home," he says to the camera. "It's a little after eight. At precisely eight o'clock I took my last sip of clean water . . . and . . . hide your eyes, Mom . . ."

He swivels the camera and reveals a bloody wound in his right forearm.

"I made an attempt—a short career in surgery, as it turned out. Those knives are just not anywhere close to the task. I've got about an inch-wide gash in my arm that goes about a half-inch deep. I cut down through the skin and the fatty tissue, and through some of the muscle. I think I cut a tendon, but I'm not sure. I tried, anyway. It really just didn't go well. The tourniquet is relaxed at this point. Which actually is a little bothersome, considering I'm not bleeding that bad, barely at all. It's so weird. You'd expect to definitely see more pulsing and bleeding, but oh well."

Aron stops the tape. He can't move the chock stone. He can't cut through his arm bones. Now he's really depressed. He wonders which threat will actually be the one to finish him off—dehydration, hypothermia, a flash flood, toxins from his dying hand, or infection from the new wound in his arm.

1:30 p.m.
Aron is out of options. He's waiting for death.
He decides it's time for another prayer.
"God, it's Aron again. I still need your help. It's getting bad here. I'm out of water and food. I know I'm going to die soon, but I want to go naturally. I've decided that regardless of what I might go through, I don't want to take my own life. It occurred to me that I could, but that's not the way I want to go. As it is, I don't figure I'll live another day—it's been three days already—I don't figure I'll see Wednesday noon. But please, God, grant me the steadfastness not to do anything against my being."
He's resolved to hang on until the bitter end.

Wednesday, 4 a.m.
Aron has rigged a kind of chair from his climbing gear, but if he sits in it for more than a few minutes it cuts off the circulation in his legs. Otherwise, he stands. He can't sleep. He's been awake since Friday night.
He does, however, enter into a series of trances. In front of the boulder, he sees a man in a white robe motion for him to follow. Aron presses on the sandstone wall, and it swings open like a gate. He steps into a living room filled with friends at a dinner party. He can see them, and they can see him, but they can't interact physically.
What's going on? he thinks. *What's happening to me here? Am I inside my head? Am I dreaming? How can that be, if I'm not sleeping? But how is this possible if it's not a dream?*
Aron is racked by spasms of cold. He's back in the canyon, his hand still trapped by the boulder. The night grinds on. In each new vision, he's no longer aware of cold or pain or hunger or thirst. But each trance ends with convulsions and the reality of the canyon.

---

11 p.m.

Aron is freezing. Even the slightest breeze leaves him shivering uncontrollably.

He begins carving on the sandstone wall above his left shoulder. When he's done, the rock reveals his final message to the world: ARON. OCT 75. APR 03. RIP.

Thursday, 10:30 a.m.

Inexplicably, Aron is still alive, though barely. He's been drinking his own urine, and it's eroding the inside of his mouth. His lips are horribly chapped. He's still wearing his contact lenses; every blink hurts. He weighed about 175 pounds on Saturday. Who knows what he weighs now?

He's beyond exhaustion, beyond everything. Waiting for the inevitable is the worst part of all.

Yesterday, he picked up a rock and pounded at the boulder, with small effect. He reaches again for the rock. His left hand is already raw from yesterday's effort. Now each blow brings on new agony.

Finally, Aron stops and puts the rock down. Dirt and bits of sandstone cover his right arm. With his multitool knife, he brushes some off. He accidentally nicks himself, exposing a section of decomposed flesh. He understands that his right hand is already dead.

Curious explorer to the end, he punctures the skin on his right thumb. It hisses; a stench rises to his nose.

Suddenly, Aron has had it. This dying appendage is no longer part of him. It's poison. It's garbage. He hates it.

Throw it away, Aron. Be rid of it.

The amazing cool he's maintained so carefully for the last five days is finally used up. He's enraged. He's screaming. He yanks again and again with his right arm, smashing his fading body against the walls of his familiar trap. His contortions force his right arm to bend at a strange angle.

Aron stops. His fury has provided an epiphany. If he applies enough force, he can bend his arm so far that the bones will break.

That's it!

There is no analysis or reflection. Aron immediately crouches as low as he can beneath the boulder, putting tension on his forearm, pushing, pushing harder still.

A popping sound from his arm echoes up the canyon walls.

Seconds later, Aron repeats his violent dance with the boulder and produces a second popping noise. He's successfully broken the radius and ulna bones in his forearm. He's excited and sweating hard. He's also in pain, but he's not thinking about that. After days of forced immobility, he's focused only on action.

Clutching his multitool, Aron tackles his next grisly task—separating his body from his decaying wrist and hand. After nearly an hour of twisting and cutting, with a break to apply his makeshift tourniquet, he makes the final slice.

Aron is overwhelmed by an ecstasy he's never known. It is a second birth.

I AM FREE!

3:00 p.m.

Despite the tourniquet and layers of clothes wrapped to make a bandage, blood is dripping steadily from Aron's right arm. He's rappelled down six stories to a waterhole in Blue John Canyon and hiked six miles through punishing heat to this point in Horseshoe Canyon. He has only two miles to go to reach the trailhead where he parked his truck five days ago, but the hike includes a steep rise at the end, and his energy is nearly gone. The outcome of his ordeal is still very much in doubt.

132

Aron follows a left turn on the trail. Seventy yards ahead is a sight so unbelievable that he wonders if it's real. Three people, two adults and a child, are on the trail. They are walking away.

Twice, Aron tries to shout, but he can't get any words out of his parched throat. Then comes a feeble sound, followed by a stronger one: "Help! HELP!"

The trio stops and turns around. Then they start running in his direction.

Aron nearly begins to cry. He's no longer alone.

He's going to live.

Would You? Could You?

(Share your answers if you're reading in a group)

Aron Ralston has been praised and criticized for his actions during the last days of April 2003. Many consider him a hero and an inspiration. One woman sent him a letter, saying, "I had promised myself that I would end my life if things had not gotten better one year after my husband's death. I know now that suicide is not the answer. You inspire me to stay strong, remain brave, and fight for life." Others point to his narrow escapes on previous adventures and his failure to leave word of his plans and conclude that he is foolish. One book reviewer said, "Aron Ralston has a death wish."

Whatever your take on Aron Ralston, it appears that when he faced the greatest challenge of his life, he found the courage and motivation to meet it. Despite truly desperate circumstances, he kept his composure and endured until a solution presented itself—and then had the fortitude to follow through on his opportunity to escape.

Life is a precious gift. How much does yours mean to you?

- *Would you* cut off a limb to save your life? If you were stuck in Aron Ralston's shoes, *could you* work out the necessary steps to stay alive and rescue yourself?

- How did Aron demonstrate his courage most—by refusing to panic, by rejecting thoughts of suicide, or by breaking his forearm bones and cutting off his hand?
- Aron has named love as the source of his courage, saying, "We're tapping into that source of strength and courage when we feel love, and we do it for our families and our friends and hopefully for the world at large. Those opportunities are out there all the time, and hopefully we're doing it for that instead of just our own egos." Is love the source of everyone's courage? If God is love (1 John 4:8), is this another way of saying that God is the source of our courage?
- After the accident, Aron continued to take risks. He completed his goal of solo-climbing the fourteen-thousand-foot peaks of Colorado. Yet he sounds changed by his encounter in the canyon, saying, "I still do like adventures. But it's different. It's not coming from an esteem-building, need-fulfillment place, like my life won't amount to something if I'm not the first person to make some major accomplishment." What do you think he means? How would such an experience change you?
- Aron has written that if he could travel back in time to Blue John Canyon in 2003, he would still go through it all again. Why might he feel this way?
- Aron's escape happened at just the right time. If he'd left a day or two earlier, he might easily have bled to death while hiking back in a deserted canyon. If he'd waited another day for rescuers to find him, he likely would have died from dehydration. Was it coincidence that caused him to find a solution at just the right moment?

Reporting In

Are you feeling trapped in any area of your life? Is there a hard choice you need to make to escape? Pray about it with the Lord.

Hitting the Trail

(This is just for you)

Before the accident, Aron Ralston had quit his job as an engineer and moved to Aspen to pursue outdoor adventures. Sonja Ralston Elder, Aron's sister, said, "What happened to him has vindicated this choice about doing what you love and not being defined by other people's expectations."

Most of us live, often unconsciously, with the expectations of others in our heads—those of our friends, parents, co-workers, and society in general. Who is defining your life?

• Make a list of the activities you're involved in, whether they are jobs, hobbies, volunteer work, or something else. Why do you participate in each?

_____

_____

_____

• How would your list change if you paid no attention to the expectations of others?

_____

_____

_____

• How important is it to weigh the opinions of others before we act, especially if the "other" is a spouse, child, or anyone who might be affected by what we do? Where does God fit into this equation? Read John 14:23–24 and record your response here.

_____

_____

_____

New Territory

(For those who want to explore further)

Read *Desert Solitaire*, Edward Abbey's reflections on a season as a park ranger near Moab, Utah, and *Into the Wild*, Jon Krakauer's account of the travels and death of young Chris McCandless in the Alaskan wilderness.

- What do we have to gain from spending time alone in the desert or wilderness?
- In what ways can you relate to Aron Ralston, Edward Abbey, and Chris McCandless? In what ways are you entirely different?

11

Terror in Tanzania

You are my hiding place; you will protect me from trouble.

Psalm 32:7

The brochure for Tanzania Adventures Inc. begins like this: "*Africa . . .* If you love wild places, even the name sends shivers of excitement up your spine. It is a place of mystery, ancient traditions, legends, and dreams."

For thirty-seven-year-old Melissa Neugebauer and her family—her husband, parents, and two young boys—her seventeen days in Tanzania have been all of that. From the time she was ten, Melissa was getting up before sunrise to join her dad in hunts on their north Texas ranch. She's hunted all her life. This safari, however, is beyond anything she's experienced before. She has camped in the African wild, mingled with the native Masai tribesmen, and of course stalked the plentiful big game in this exotic land on the continent's eastern shore. Today, August 13, 2008, she seeks one of the most formidable creatures on the planet: the mighty Cape buffalo.

For Leon Lamprecht, thirty-nine, the past two and a half weeks have been enjoyable routine. He has patiently stalked game with Melissa's boys and led hunts with Melissa, her husband, and her father. The son of a South African game warden, Leon qualified as a professional hunter at the age of twenty-one and is licensed in three African nations. He's also served as a platoon commander in the South African Infantry Corps. Leon has seen just about everything during his years in the wild. Yet neither he nor Melissa can anticipate what awaits them this day.

After a breakfast of yogurt, fruit, bacon, and eggs at their Rungwa Ikili camp, Melissa and Leon, along with two trackers and a game warden, climb into a Toyota Land Cruiser and drive north. The weather is perfect: seventy-five degrees and sunny. At 9:45, they find fresh buffalo tracks crossing the road. For over an hour, they stalk a small herd across several miles of rough terrain. Finally, the herd comes into view. One is a handsome bull with deeply curved horns. He must weigh at least fifteen hundred pounds. But to the disappointment of the trackers, Melissa decides to let him go. Though mature, he's still young. She'll let him share his amazing genes a while longer. Besides, she has a feeling there is something else in store for her this day.

At about 3:30 in the afternoon, one of the trackers glimpses a large, lone Cape buffalo heading past a ten-foot-tall termite mound into the *miombo* (Swahili for a dry wooded area). Leon parks the vehicle downwind, and the group backtracks, looking for signs of the buffalo. They can't find a trace, so they walk to the termite mound and begin tracking into the *miombo*, this time with the wind at their backs. It puts the hunters at a disadvantage; the buffalo may catch their scent before they spot him.

Slowly, the group proceeds. The trackers are in front, followed by Leon, then Melissa, then the game warden. They are spread out, each a few feet apart from the closest companion. Leon carries his weapon—a Krieghoff double rifle—casually, against his shoulder. He's crouched, studying the ground, more intent on finding signs of the buffalo than preparing to shoot it. Most of the grass has been burned away by a fire, but much of the ground is still covered by fallen leaves. Ring-necked turtle doves call in the distance; otherwise, in the heat of the afternoon, all is quiet.

Suddenly, there is a rustling and the sound of feet pounding through the leaves. Leon looks up. The two trackers are crashing through the brush, heading right. Behind them, only twenty paces away, something black and deadly bears down on Leon. It's the buffalo, five feet tall and probably sixteen hundred pounds, his nose in the air, charging at full speed.

It all happens so quickly. Leon stands. There is movement behind him—Melissa. The buffalo is attracted to the motion and veers in that direction.

Leon has the rifle in his hands now, but there's no time to raise it to his shoulder. The buffalo is already on top of him. Leon is overwhelmed by a sense of hopelessness. The buffalo is thundering right next to him. Leon can hear, from behind, the game warden shouting, "*Piga! Piga!*" ("Shoot! Shoot!"). With the rifle at his hip, Leon points at the bull's shoulder and fires.

And then the buffalo is past, still charging.

At the sound of commotion, Melissa had looked up and seen the scattering trackers. In the next instant, she realized the buffalo was charging.

Shoot! was her first thought. But her rifle is on a strap on her shoulder. *Tree!* entered her mind next. But the bull is less than ten yards away.

Melissa turns, hears the bellow of Leon's Krieghoff, sees that there are no climbable trees. She runs three or four steps, then grabs the thin branch of a sapling as if to protect herself.

Too late. She feels a blow against her hip. She is being thrust into the air.

Leon is amazed and horrified to see Melissa's body flip up on top of the bull. Her stomach is pressed against the boss of his horns, her head above his neck, legs clad in khaki cargo pants dangling over his eyes and nose. On any other buffalo, she might have been gored by the sharp tips of the horns. But this bull's horns have an unusual shape. Instead of dropping down from the boss and curling back into dangerous points, they extend almost straight out, then curve in on themselves. Because of that extra curl, Melissa is safe from the pointed tips while atop the buffalo's head, but she's pinned between the curves of his horns.

The bull doesn't like any of this. He runs into the brush for several yards, shaking his head violently the entire time.

Leon runs after him. He isn't really thinking; he's acting on autopilot. He knows that somehow he's got to help Melissa before it's too late.

The buffalo stops and lowers his head. Melissa tumbles from atop the bull onto the ground, where she rolls to a stop.

Melissa is on her belly. She presses her face into the dirt, covers her head with her hands, and kicks her legs out straight. She's trying to be as small and narrow as possible. She knows it's not going to do any good.

Oh my gosh, she thinks. *This is about to hurt.*

The enraged buffalo steps over Melissa. The earth trembles when his feet pound the ground on both sides of her body. She feels the wind of his breath against her back and smells a thick, potent animal odor.

The bull stomps past, then returns, slamming his head into the ground next to Melissa. He's trying to squash her with the boss on top of his head, but the curved horns strike the ground first, preventing him from landing a blow.

The buffalo lunges again.

Leon doesn't want to somehow shoot Melissa by accident, so he moves closer, standing just a few feet away from the buffalo. He aims his rifle at the bull's neck, hoping to break its spine. He pulls the trigger.

Nothing happens.

The buffalo turns. He comes at Leon. Quickly, the hunter targets the buffalo's head and fires.

Again, nothing.

What Leon doesn't realize is that during the chaos of the buffalo's first charge, he'd pulled the rear trigger of his Krieghoff instead of the front trigger. Now, believing he's already shot from the front trigger barrel, he's still attempting to fire the empty second chamber.

It no longer matters; the bull is charging. Leon raises his rifle in front of him, feeling like a matador with a cape. Just before impact, he sees the buffalo's eyes roll back, the eye sockets turning milky white, in sharp contrast against the blackness of the beast's face.

The bull hits the rifle first and shakes his head. Leon's left hand is briefly caught between the rifle and a horn. His thumb splits open; he can feel pain in his hand and wrist. The Krieghoff flies into the air to the right. Leon is tossed to the left, but he keeps his feet.

The buffalo has run past. Now he stops and turns in the direction of the rifle. Leon moves with him, the improvising matador, trying to stay behind the bull. If only he can reach his rifle.

Melissa is thinking about her own rifle. She raises her head and sees Leon dancing with the bull. She sees her weapon lying about five feet away in the dirt.

I need to grab my gun and shoot it, she thinks. *It's right there.*

She starts to lift herself off the ground.

"No, Melissa!" Leon yells. He puts his arm out as if to hold her there. "Lay still! Don't move!"

Melissa drops back down and again covers her head.

As he circles behind the buffalo, Leon scoops up his rifle. He realizes *both* his hands are mangled and bloody; his right thumb was injured during the first shot from the hip at the bull. Even so, he is able to reload while on the move.

The buffalo, perhaps sensing that his time is up, suddenly runs in Melissa's direction. But he doesn't stop to crush her prone figure. He roars past toward the Tanzanian bush.

Leon fires his rifle, this time getting off a shot. But the volley is high. The game warden, who had run for cover initially, is back on the scene. He also fires, but the buffalo does not slow down. Soon the bull is out of sight.

Leon, feeling a flood of relief as well as frustration at not being able to prevent the attack, helps Melissa to her feet. Incredibly, though she is badly scraped in places, she has no major injuries. The buffalo neither stabbed her nor stepped on her.

Just then, Melissa's father and another hunter drive up in another Land Cruiser. Leon is sure he hit the buffalo with his first shot, so Leon and the hunter go after the supposedly wounded buffalo. They never find him.

Melissa is evacuated on a medical plane and taken to a Nairobi hospital. She is bruised and scratched, but she has no broken bones or internal injuries. There's no room for Leon on the flight, so he's treated in camp and driven to a hospital the next day. His right thumb is dislocated, and his left hand has a few small broken bones—a small price to pay for a faceoff with a Cape buffalo.

The circumstances that allowed Melissa and Leon to escape serious injury still amaze them both. Melissa is a petite five feet two inches, 105 pounds. If she'd been any other size, she would not have fit exactly within the unusual curves of the Cape buffalo's horns. Any larger or smaller and she could easily have slid off and been trampled. The fact that the buffalo's hooves repeatedly stomped over and around Melissa without actually landing on her is equally improbable. And it was only the unique shape of the bull's horns that prevented him from goring or squashing Melissa. Leon, meanwhile, took the brunt of the buffalo's charge and suffered only the damage to his left hand.

And then there is the fanny pack. On the day before the hunt, Melissa's son Noah, eight years old, handed her his fanny pack, saying, "Here Mommy, you keep this. You might need it." It was filled with tissue paper, sanitary wipes, crackers, and a compass. Melissa decided to wear it for the hunt. When the buffalo struck her on the hip, he hit the one spot where Melissa had a bit of padding—the fanny pack.

To Melissa and Leon, both people of faith, the only explanation for so many coincidences is providence.

"I'm sure the Lord has protected me a thousand times throughout my life in ways I never even knew about, but that day he made his protection quite evident," Melissa says. "I will live the rest of the days he gives me thanking him for every breath."

Would You? Could You?

(Share your answers if you're reading in a group)

Teddy Roosevelt, a man who reveled in the African safari as much as anyone, once said, "It is not the critic who counts: not the man who points out how the strong man stumbles or where the doer of deeds could have done better. The credit belongs to the man who is actually in the arena, whose face is marred by dust and sweat and blood, who strives valiantly, who errs and comes up short again and again, because there is no effort without error or shortcoming, but who knows the great enthusiasms, the great devotions, who spends himself for a worthy cause; who, at the best, knows, in the end, the triumph of high achievement, and who, at the worst, if he fails, at least he fails while daring greatly, so that his place shall never be with those cold and timid souls who knew neither victory nor defeat."

Part of the allure of the hunt is the chance to test oneself in the arena, to strive valiantly while tasting dust and sweat and blood. Melissa Neugebauer and Leon Lamprecht had spent their lives facing such tests, but they never encountered anything quite like the charging Cape buffalo in Tanzania. In many ways, both performed admirably that afternoon. They kept clear heads, they responded well to changing and deadly circumstances, and they did not try to do more than what they were capable of. Leon, in particular, showed great courage in keeping the bull away from Melissa. Though the buffalo got away, Melissa and Leon both experienced the "triumph of high achievement." It could be argued that the regular testing they put themselves through, in the form of the demands of the hunt, enabled them to pass their greatest test.

There is a fine line here when danger is involved. Those who continually enter the arena, pushing themselves to greater and greater challenges, can fail spectacularly—and fatally. Those who continually avoid the arena, on the other hand, are ill-prepared when the great test does arrive. They are among the cold and timid souls who draw Roosevelt's scorn.

So how about you? Are you a critic or a man of credit? A timid soul or a case for courage? If you were in Leon Lamprecht's boots and a Cape buffalo was threatening your client, *would you* run forward or run for cover?

- Mark Twain once said that "Courage is resistance to fear, mastery of fear—not absence of fear." Despite his experience as a hunter, guide, and infantryman, Leon was not immune to fluster. In those first critical moments, he pulled the wrong trigger on his rifle. Yet his actions in the moments that followed may well have saved Melissa Neugebauer's life. *Could you* have been as coolheaded and courageous as Leon during a similar crisis?

- What do you think was the source of Leon's courage? Was it his experience? An ability to control his emotions? His sense of responsibility? What gives you courage?
- Some people, such as Leon, choose to make courageous decisions in an instant. Others are paralyzed by crisis; yet when given time to think matters through, they will also make a courageous choice—for example, quitting a job to preserve their integrity. What is the difference between the two kinds of courage? Are you more likely to enact one over the other? Why?
- The tally of coincidences that Melissa and Leon experienced on their hunt is remarkable. What do you think about the nature of coincidence? Is there a point where coincidence stops and God starts?
- After the incident, Melissa's mother said that angels must have been protecting her daughter. Leon says he knows angels have protected him in the past. He and others prayed for protection before the safari with Melissa's family, and he's sure angels protected him from the charging buffalo. Do you believe in angels and the power of God's protection?
- Read the account of Jesus and Peter walking on water in Matthew 14:22–36. Does this imply a link between courage and faith? How important is faith to a person's courage? To yours? Do people of genuine faith have an advantage in crisis situations?

Reporting In

Is the Lord calling you to act with greater courage in any area of your life? Take time now to talk with him about it.

Hitting the Trail

(This is just for you)

An African safari may not be in your short-term vacation plans, but we all can find other ways to test ourselves in the arena and develop our courage. And aren't we most useful to God when we are ready to act with strength and courage on his behalf? Maybe it's not coincidence that you're reading this story today. Maybe the Lord is trying to encourage you to boldly move into the purpose he's designed just for you.

- Make a list of your greatest fears. What does this say about your courage? What does it say about your faith?

  _____

  _____

  _____

- Do you think you could take steps to decrease these fears and increase your courage? What would have to change in your life to make that happen? Is prayer and time in the Word part of the equation? Write down your thoughts here.

  _____

  _____

  _____

- Imagine how God might use you if you had more courage, whether that would involve a job change, a lifestyle change, starting or ending a relationship, taking that short-term missions trip, or something else. Write down what that might look like. Ask the Lord if this is part of his plan for you—and if so, what you should do next.

_____

_____

_____

New Territory

(For those who want to explore further)

Read a biography or two about Teddy Roosevelt, America's twenty-sixth president, such as Donald Brinkley's *The Wilderness Warrior: Theodore Roosevelt and the Crusade for America.*

- What do you think attracted Roosevelt to hunting and the wilderness?
- What was the source of Roosevelt's courage as a hunter, cavalryman, and president? When did he demonstrate the greatest courage? How is courage an important quality for leadership?

12

End of the Rope

You must do the thing which you think you cannot do.

Eleanor Roosevelt

On a sunny afternoon in June 1985, two men clad in heavy winter gear stand together at the summit cornice of Siula Grande, a forbidding, twenty-one-thousand-foot peak in the Peruvian Andes. After three days of hard climbing, they've achieved the first ascent of the mountain's sheer west face and celebrated with photos and chocolate. Now comes the hard part—getting down.

The two Brits have been climbing together since meeting in the French Alps the year before. Twenty-one-year-old Simon Yates is tall and strong, with blond hair and blue eyes. He has a degree in biochemistry, but his passion is adventure in the mountains. His partner, twenty-four-year-old Joe Simpson, is shorter and powerful as well, with dark brown hair and a square jaw. He shares Yates's passion for climbing.

Yates has been checking out their expected line of descent along the north ridge. He's also watching the weather. "Looks like we are in for another storm," he says.

Simpson turns to look as well. Clouds are rising from the east face and expanding to the west.

"It looks hairy," Simpson says.

"Yeah. Better get our skates on. If we move quickly, we can traverse under that summit and then rejoin the ridge farther down. In fact, I don't think we'll even have an hour."

Yates is right. Forty minutes later, it's snowing hard. The climbers are descending in the midst of a whiteout. It's slow and dangerous work. When darkness falls, Simpson digs a snow cave, and they rest for the night. It's bitterly cold, at least twenty degrees below zero. Two of Yates's fingers are developing frostbite.

At 7:30 the next morning, the climbers begin descending again. By midmorning they are down to only twenty thousand feet, but they keep at it. Simpson leads and keeps falling into crevasses up to his eyes, each slip punctuated by a series of shouts and curses. Despite their risky position, Yates can't help grinning as he watches his partner's comical struggles.

A short time later, Simpson is hidden behind a rise in the ridge when Yates feels a violent yank on the rope between them. He's dragged forward several feet until he halts the motion by thrusting his ice axes into the snow. He knows Simpson has fallen. Ten minutes later, the rope goes slack.

Yates climbs over the rise, wondering what went wrong. He peers down and sees Simpson with his left foot dug into the slope, his face hidden by the snow.

"What happened?" Yates says. "Are you okay?"

Simpson is startled. He looks up. "I fell. The edge gave way." He adds in a controlled, flat voice, "I've broken my leg."

Yates immediately recognizes the significance of Simpson's words. He also understands the look of doom on his partner's face. They both know there's no way down this massif with a bum leg.

"Are you sure it's broken?"

"Yes."

Yates's first thoughts are coldly rational and inescapable. *You're dead . . . no two ways about it.*

Yates climbs down. He sees the frightening twist of Simpson's right knee and gives him a few pain pills. He can't think of anything to say, so he stays silent.

Their ropes are jammed, so Yates must climb the crest of the ridge to free them. It's the hardest climbing he has ever done. Nearly everything he touches collapses and disappears down the west face. When he finally reaches the top, Yates is shaking from fear and fatigue.

He looks down and is amazed to see Simpson traversing slowly to the west. Below him are thousands of feet of open air. It's a pitiful sight. Simpson buries his axes in the snow, then makes a tiny hop on his good leg.

He'll probably fall, Yates thinks. *In a way, I hope he does. I can't leave him while he's still fighting for it, but I have no idea how to help him. If I try to get him down, I might die with him. It seems a waste.*

Yates moves down to Simpson's position, then traverses ahead of him. From here he can see the col, followed by the long, steep west face that leads to the glacier and their base camp six miles beyond. It's about six hundred feet to the col.

Simpson eventually catches up. Yates puts a hand on his shoulder. "How're you doing?"

"It's better. Painful, but . . . I've had it, Simon. I can't see myself getting down at this rate."

Yates says nothing and begins untying the rope from its harness.

Then Simpson gets an idea. "Do you think you can hold my weight in this snow?" he asks. They're out of snow stakes. If Yates attempts lowering Simpson down the slope, he'll do so with no anchors to secure his own position.

"If we dig a bucket seat, I should be able to hold you," Yates says. "If it starts to collapse, I can always shout and you can take your weight off."

The agreement is made. Their ropes are tied into a single, three-hundred-foot line. Yates will lower Simpson on the rope and use a belay plate to control the speed of the descent. Each time they reach the knot between the two ropes, Simpson will need to stand up on the slope, taking his weight off the rope so Yates can move the knot to the other side of the belay plate.

Yates digs a deep hole in the snow and sits in it, facing away from the slope. He takes hold of the rope and braces his legs against the fresh snow barrier. It's the only thing that will keep them both from tumbling off the mountain.

"Okay," Yates says. "You ready?"

"Yes. Now take it steady. If anything slips, yell."

"Don't worry, I will. If you can't hear me when the knot comes up, I'll tug the rope three times."

"Right."

Yates nods and grins, and they're off. The system works. After two lowerings, they are able to traverse to the col. The three-thousand-foot descent down the treacherous west face remains, however. It's four o'clock, and the clouds are massing again. The pair briefly considers spending the night where they are.

"I think we should keep going," Yates finally says. "Will you be all right?"

"Yes. Let's go. I'm freezing."

They continue, working efficiently, as if they've always descended this way. Speed is essential, so Yates drops Simpson quickly, though he knows each bounce against the slope shoots indescribable pain through Simpson's leg. There is the pause to change the knot, then Yates climbs down when they reach the end of the rope. At first, Simpson is able to finish digging a bucket seat for Yates by the time he arrives after a lowering. Because of the increasing cold and their fatigue, however, Simpson accomplishes less and less of the seat each time.

Yates's own fingers are getting worse. The last time he looked, four fingertips and one thumb were black.

152

It quickly grows dark, and small avalanches pour over the climbers. Yates encourages Simpson as he settles into yet another hole in the snow.

"Two lowers to go at the most, I reckon," he says. "This will be the eighth, plus the two abseils, so we've covered two thousand seven hundred feet, or thereabouts. It can't be more than three thousand, so this might even be the last one."

Simpson nods and half grins, half grimaces as he goes over the edge once again. Yates can hear faint cries of pain as Simpson slams against the face. Unfortunate, he thinks, but necessary.

From above, another blast of snow showers over Yates. He hunkers lower into his makeshift seat.

Suddenly, the rope jerks forward, and Yates is nearly yanked off the mountain. He throws himself backward and brakes with his legs. The harness digs into his hips, the rope taut between his legs.

They're too far apart and there's too much wind to hear each other. Yates waits thirty minutes, holding Simpson's weight, but there's no change, no tugging on the rope to indicate he's trying to climb up. The bucket seat has crumbled to half its original size. Yates doesn't have the leverage or the strength to haul Simpson back up. He has no choice but to lower him farther and hope he'll find solid footing.

Yates releases the rope again. The knot appears twenty feet below. There's still no change in the rope's tension.

What am I lowering him over?

Yates stamps his feet, trying to get better purchase in his snow hole. Another small avalanche hits him from behind, filling in the space behind him, pushing him closer to the edge.

Could he hold the rope with one hand and move the knot above the plate with the other? Yates lifts one hand off the rope. His tortured fingers can't even make a fist. No good.

Nearly an hour after they began the lower, Yates is frozen and shaking. His hold on the rope keeps slipping a few inches at a time, until the knot is tight against his right fist. Yates is losing strength.

I can't hold it. I can't stop it.

More of the seat beneath him collapses. His body slides forward a few inches. Soon, Simpson's weight will pull them both off the mountain.

I have to do something!

The thought strikes him suddenly.

The knife! Of course, the knife. Be quick, come on, get it.

Nearly panicked, Yates uses one hand to carefully slide off one strap, then the other, of the rucksack on his back. He reaches in, feeling for the knife, as more of the snow seat crumbles. He discovers something smooth and pulls it out. Yates drops the knife in his lap and pulls off a glove with his teeth.

He's already decided. He has no choice.

He holds the knife in one hand and opens the blade with his teeth. The cold metal sticks to his lips.

Yates reaches toward the rope with his knife, then stops.

The slack rope! Clear the loose rope twisted round my foot! If it tangled, it would rip me down with it.

Yates moves the rope and checks with his eyes to make sure everything is clear. Again, he stretches the knife toward the taut rope. He touches the blade against it.

The rope explodes.

With the tension suddenly released, Yates slams back against the snow behind him. He's shaking and breathing fast, his heart pounding. Snow falls over him and down his neck.

Have I killed him?

He feels no guilt or sorrow, only emptiness.

He's alone in the cold on the steep slope of a killer mountain. There is nothing else to be done except build a snow cave.

During the night, Yates is tormented by questions. He finds himself wondering about his motives, or at least thinking he ought to question them.

I'm satisfied with myself, he thought. *I'm actually pleased I was strong enough to cut the rope. There was nothing else left for me, so I went ahead with it. I did it, and did it well. That takes some doing! A lot of people would die before getting it together to do that! I'm still alive because I held everything together right up to the last moment . . .*

But what of Joe?

In the morning, Yates is filled with dread. He knows Simpson is dead. He expects to die on the descent as well. He's calm and grim when he reaches the point where Simpson would have been hanging on the rope. He's shocked to see a towering ice cliff, fifty feet at least. It all feels cruel and sickening.

Yates descends to a crevasse in the glacier beneath the face. The closer he gets, the more he realizes its depth. No one could survive a fall into that.

"Joe!"

The only response is the echo of his voice.

Yates turns away. There's no point in looking closer. He has to face the truth. Head down, he trudges on toward base camp and their friend Richard, far below. On the long walk, he argues with himself.

Why tell them you cut the rope? They'll never know otherwise, so what difference does it make! Just say he fell down a crevasse when we were coming down the glacier. Yeah! Tell them we were unroped.

When Yates runs into Richard on the path to camp, however, he doesn't lie. He can't say Simpson carelessly fell into a crevasse, not after all his struggle. It would be an injustice. He tells the whole story.

Yates, physically and emotionally exhausted, spends the next day recovering. On the following day, Richard is ready to break camp and return to Lima. But Yates doesn't feel ready to leave. At first, he tells Richard to go on ahead, that he'll catch up in a few days. Finally, however, they agree to depart together in the morning.

It's snowing and nearly 1 a.m. when Yates, in the tent, hears the ghostly howl.

"Siiimmmooonnn."

Not possible.

A few moments later, the voice calls out again: "Help meeeee!"

Yates, eyes wide, grabs a flashlight and stumbles into the snow, Richard behind him.

"Joe! Is that you? JOE!" Yates's voice cracks with emotion. He hears sobbing, heads for the sound.

The flashlight beam reveals a thin body, its clothes tattered. It's Simpson. He's alive.

Hours later, after being filled with hot tea, an exhausted Simpson describes falling 150 feet onto a snow bridge in the crevasse, lowering himself deeper into the crevasse until he found a new way to climb out, and then the desperate, six-mile hop and crawl, part of it through a blizzard, down the glacier to base camp. It took three and a half days.

Simpson, alone with Yates in the tent, has one more thing to add before falling into a blessed sleep.

"You saved my life, you know. It must have been terrible for you that night. I don't blame you. You had no choice. I understand that, and I understand why you thought I was dead. You did all that you could have done. Thanks for getting me down."

Once again, Yates has no words. But the tears on his cheeks say all that needs to be said.

Would You? Could You?

(Share your answers if you're reading in a group)

In the years since their climb in the Andes, Simon Yates's decision to cut his tether to Joe Simpson has been the subject of considerable debate. Once he remembered he had a knife, Yates says it was an instant and intuitive decision, one that "felt the right thing to do." He adds, "Ultimately, we all have to look after ourselves, whether on mountains or in day-to-day life. In my view that is not a license to be selfish, for only by taking good care of ourselves are we able to help others. Away from the mountains, in the complexity of everyday life, the price of neglecting this responsibility might be a marriage breaking down, a disruptive child, a business failing, or a house repossessed. In the mountains the penalty for neglect can often be death."

Contrast this view with the true story told by Patrick Morley of a father and his twelve-year-old son, trapped with two other fishermen on a sinking seaplane in a secluded Alaskan bay. All jumped into the water and swam for shore. The fishermen made it and turned around to see the father arm in arm with his son, floating out to sea. They were sure the father was a strong enough swimmer to reach shore. They surmised that the son wasn't. The father chose to die with his son rather than save himself.

It takes courage to make hard choices, especially when the consequences are life or death. Simon Yates and the father described above made their choices. What will you choose?

- If you were in the same position as Simon Yates, *would you* cut the rope and let your partner fall? *Could you* do it, knowing your partner would likely die? For that matter, *could you* hang on till the end, knowing it would probably cost you your life?
- Yates says we have a responsibility to take care of ourselves and acted accordingly. The father in the Alaskan bay probably felt he was fulfilling his responsibility too. Whose actions were right—or were they both right? Is there a right answer in such situations?
- Was it courage, a sense of responsibility, survival instinct, or something else that allowed Yates to cut the rope?
- Joe Simpson cites Yates's bravery in helping him with the dangerous descent after he broke his leg. Yates writes of

his decision to continue climbing and to carry on with life as before, even though he was "now truly aware of the ultimate penalty that mountaineering could exact." Is Yates a brave man? Which act took greater courage? Why?

- Simpson describes himself as an atheist and says that if he believed in God in the Andes, he probably would have stopped struggling and died waiting for God to rescue him. Is God this kind of rescuer? Why or why not?
- Simpson has also talked about feeling an overwhelming sense of loneliness and abandonment in the Andes. He did not want to die alone. The Bible says, "Be strong and courageous. Do not be terrified; do not be discouraged, for the LORD your God will be with you wherever you go" (Josh. 1:9). If Simpson had been a believer, how might it have affected his loneliness?

Reporting In

Do you feel God's presence on a daily basis? Spend time with him right now and confess whatever is testing your courage.

Hitting the Trail

(This is just for you)

We've been exploring the topic of courage in some of the most extreme circumstances imaginable. But the depth of a man's or woman's courage can be measured just as well, perhaps even more so, in the everyday challenges of life. The husband who sticks by his wife after she has an affair . . . the single mother who quietly battles cancer . . . the teenager who stays faithful even when friends reject him for his beliefs—these also demand a special brand of courage.

It's time to take stock. Are you strong and courageous?

- What are the daily challenges and circumstances that strike fear in your heart? Are you meeting them with courage or finding ways to hold back?

  _____

  _____

  _____

- What can you do to bolster your courage? How can the Lord help?

  _____

  _____

  _____

- Who are the bravest people in your life? What are the secrets to their courage? If you don't know the answer, how can you find out?

  _____

  _____

  _____

New Territory

(For those who want to explore further)

Read Joe Simpson's *Touching the Void*, his account of his adventure in the Andes. Watch the movie of the same name.

- When does Joe Simpson demonstrate his greatest courage?
- Why are Simpson and Yates driven to continually test their mortality in the mountains?

159

PART FOUR

LEADERSHIP

13

The Expedition

He who has compassion on them will guide
them and lead them beside springs of water.

Isaiah 49:10

Standing on an Antarctic ice floe, his breath appearing
in small clouds of white, Ernest Shackleton watches his
men feed their sled dogs. A movement in the distance
catches his eye.

It is the *Endurance*—and she is sinking. The stout Norwegian schooner has carried Shackleton and his twenty-seven
crew members thirteen thousand miles to this forlorn spot
in the Weddell Sea. They are only one day's sail from their
intended destination, Antarctica's Vashel Bay, from which
Shackleton had hoped to launch the first overland expedition
across the continent.

But five months after departing England in the summer
of 1914, the *Endurance* was thwarted by an unusually severe
winter and trapped in the polar ice. No amount of effort
could free her. For the past ten months, Shackleton and his

mates have endured in the subzero conditions as they waited for their frozen prison to release them.

The wait was in vain. A few weeks earlier, the vise grip around the *Endurance* tightened; she was being crushed by ice. The men were forced to abandon ship. Now their lone symbol of civilization is disappearing—and with it the faint hope of restoring their former home.

"She's going, boys!" Shackleton shouts. He dashes up a lookout tower. The crew scrambles out of tents pitched on the frozen wasteland and watches silently. Across the ice pack, the stern of *Endurance* rises twenty feet into the air, her propeller and rudder clearly visible. Then, slowly, she is devoured by the sea. Less than ten minutes after Shackleton's shout, there is no trace of the schooner. Ice closes up the black hole of open water that marked her grave.

The sight is heartbreaking for all. Shackleton is so devastated that later, in his journal, he notes that "I cannot write about it." In front of his charges, however, Shackleton shows no sign of disappointment or loss. "Ship and stores have gone," he tells them, "so now we'll go home."

It is a typical Shackleton moment. The expedition leader is adapting to the circumstances, giving his men what they need most—confident direction delivered in a calm voice. It is not the first such moment on this journey, nor will it be the last.

From the beginning of the expedition, Shackleton has worked to mold his men into a cohesive unit. He broke down typical divisions between officers and crew, sailors and scientists, by requiring everyone to pitch in on ship's work. Seamen would take hydrographic readings. Doctors and scientists would do their share of chores, night watches, and turns at the helm. Shackleton also rotated work assignments to encourage multiple friendships and prevent cliques. The trust and camaraderie they built up soon served them well.

When the *Endurance* became trapped, Shackleton fought against anxiety, boredom, and dissension by promoting games on the ice floes: soccer, hockey, and dog races. He also continued to celebrate birthdays, holidays, and other special events. Meteorologist Leonard Hussey entertained with his banjo. Despite adversity, the men were content, even happy. They were living proof of one of Shackleton's core beliefs: "Adventure is the soul of existence because it [brings] out true harmony among men."

Then came the day the ice wrapped itself tighter around the *Endurance*, warping her sides and wringing animal-like screams from her beams. A band of emperor penguins watched the tortured ship and uttered a series of mournful cries unknown to all on board. "Do you hear that?" one crew member said. "We'll none of us get back to our homes again."

The men lowered their three lifeboats, gathered what supplies they could, and congregated on the sturdiest-looking ice floe. Shackleton could see the discouragement in their faces. He addressed the group, calmly explaining his plans and what they were up against. He rallied them with what one expedition member described as a "simple, moving, optimistic, and highly effective" speech.

After the sinking of the *Endurance*, the men at least know what they are up against. It falls to them to pull themselves out of their predicament.

The next five-and-a-half months are a sentence of useless attempts to cross the dangerous, uneven ice floes on foot, followed by endless waiting. As they wait, the ice pack gradually drifts northwest.

Finally, as the Antarctic summer moves into fall, the warmed-up ice begins to break apart. The expedition's ice floe, once a mile in diameter, is now less than two hundred yards across. The men ready the three lifeboats and hope for a channel of open water. There is no time to lose; the current is taking them away from the series of small islands along Antarctica's northwest tip and toward the open sea.

On the evening of April 8, 1916, the ice floe splits. Two boats are hurried across the crack so the group can stay together. The next morning, the floe splits again as other floes grind against it. The men watch as ice and water jockey for position. At 12:40 in the afternoon, Shackleton quietly gives the order: "Launch the boats." There is no turning back. If the ice closes again, the lifeboats will be crushed, along with any hope of survival.

In the first thirty minutes, the rowers in the three small boats make gradual progress; the ice seems to loosen further. Many are admiring a flat-top iceberg close by when a low roar attracts all eyes to starboard. Bearing down on them is a lavalike flow of tumbling ice, at least two feet high and wide as a river. It's a riptide, and it can easily sink them all.

Shackleton swings his boat around and shouts for the others to do the same. It's a race for survival. The oarsmen dig in, four in each boat, pulling with all their strength. They are facing astern, staring straight at their enemy. Twice the *Dudley Docker*, the most cumbersome boat to row, is nearly overtaken. After fifteen minutes, when the oarsmen have nearly nothing left, the riptide loses some of its fury. Five minutes later, it flattens out. Fresh rowers take over, and the boats resume their original course.

It is the beginning of seven days of misery. On the first night, the men are able to pitch tents on a floe. Shackleton takes the first watch, sleeps for an hour, then gets up again to survey the floe. He seems inexhaustible, forever watching and planning on behalf of his party.

His vigilance saves the life of crewman Ernie Holness. In the darkness, a large swell strikes the floe. "Crack!" someone yells. The split widens underneath a tent. Holness, in his sleeping bag, falls into icy water. Shackleton rushes forward, throws himself onto the edge of the ice, grabs the bag, and heaves Holness out of the water. A moment later, another swell cements the crack in the floe back together.

Later, in the boats, Captain Frank Worsley uses a sextant to determine the expedition's position. On the third day, despite rowing west, they are twenty-two miles east of their former camp on the ice—they're being swept toward open ocean. That night, when the moon peeks through the clouds, Shackleton takes stock of his men. They are wet, cold, hungry, thirsty, and exhausted from rowing and lack of sleep. Lips are cracked, eyes red, faces crusted with salt. Some are suffering the first signs of frostbite.

"In the momentary light, I could see their ghostly faces," Shackleton later wrote in his journal. "I doubted if all the men would survive the night." Yet he reveals none of his misgivings, and shouts encouragement across the water.

In the morning, all of Shackleton's desperate crew members are still alive—and they get a break. The wind rises and shifts to the southeast. Shackleton decides to run west for Elephant Island, one hundred miles to the northwest. If the wind holds, they have a chance.

For three more days, the men and their boats battle the raging sea. Shackleton works to lift the spirits of his crew. At one point, he insists that photographer Frank Hurley wear his gloves after Hurley accidentally leaves his own pair on a floe. Another time, he calls out to Perce Blackborow, a stowaway the expedition leader has come to appreciate. Blackborow has no feeling in his feet; it seems only a matter of time before gangrene sets in. "We shall be on Elephant Island tomorrow," Shackleton tells him. "No one has ever landed there before, and you will be the first ashore."

Finally, on April 16, three battered lifeboats are hauled onto a lonely beach. Shackleton tries to keep his promise, but Blackborow cannot walk; two crewmen help him ashore. Another man collapses from a heart attack, but survives. For the first time in a year and four months, the expedition is on blessed land.

It is a victory, but Shackleton and his men know they are far from safe. Elephant Island is small and remote; no whaling ships will be stopping here. Shackleton soon announces that he and a party of five will set out for the whaling stations on the island of South Georgia. It is a truly desperate bid—sailing eight hundred miles in an open lifeboat on the planet's stormiest ocean to a piece of land twenty-five miles across at its widest. But Shackleton has no choice.

Shackleton selects his crew with care, considering not only the hard voyage ahead but also the plight of those left behind. Crack navigator Worsley is an obvious choice, and sturdy second officer Tom Crean and likeable seaman Tim McCarthy are also easy decisions. Two others—carpenter Harry McNeish and seaman John Vincent—are chosen as much for their rebellious nature as for their skills. Shackleton does not want them to poison the already grim environment they will leave behind on Elephant Island.

After making improvements to the *James Caird*, at twenty-two feet the expedition's largest lifeboat, Shackleton and his small band are off. Once again, their leader does what he can to make the journey bearable. Shackleton declares that there will be no swearing and establishes a schedule for meals, rest, watches, and manning the tiller. These measures are of little solace against mounting hardships, however. Layer after layer of ice weighs down the boat. One night, Worsley is frozen in position; the others have to unfold and massage him to get him into a sleeping bag. The wet bags begin to rot. Frostbite sets in.

Shortly after midnight on May 5, Shackleton is at the tiller. The sky is overcast and a gale is blowing. Shackleton looks up, sees a band of white, and calls to the others that the sky is clearing. A moment later he hears a low roar and looks up again. He realizes that the "clearing" is actually the crest of an enormous wave.

"Hold on!" he shouts. "It's got us!"

The seawater pounds the *James Caird* and everything in it, nearly tearing Shackleton from his seat. Though instantly flooded, the boat miraculously stays afloat. The men bail for their lives, knowing that any more water will sink them. Gradually, they rise out of the ocean again.

Three days later, having beaten the incredible odds, McCarthy spies South Georgia. But before they can make a landing, a hurricane hits. The violent waves are too dangerous. With their goal only minutes away, Shackleton orders the boat back out to sea. After two more days of waiting, and with the crew's strength virtually gone, the *James Caird* makes for a small cove in the cliffs to starboard. The passage is narrow, but at 5 p.m. on May 10, Shackleton jumps ashore.

The harrowing adventure isn't over. The men have landed on the opposite side of the island from the whaling stations. They don't have the stamina for another 150-mile boat journey, nor do they want to risk being carried irretrievably into the Southern Ocean. They must attempt to cross the island—more than thirty miles of mountains, glaciers, frozen streams and lakes, and waterfalls—on foot. No one has ever done it.

At 2 a.m. on May 19, Shackleton, Worsley, and Crean set out under a full moon. Hoping to travel quickly, they carry no sleeping bags or stove. Their only climbing gear is a rope, nails hammered into their boots, and a carpenter's adze.

Three times the trio reaches the top of a ridge, only to be forced to retreat by some obstacle and search out a new path. Disheartened, they wonder if they will die here, alone in the middle of the island, after overcoming so much. Shackleton does not let them give up, however. "Come on, boys," he calls.

The sun is setting by the time the men reach the top of the fourth ridge. It is a steep, nine-hundred-foot slope down. They fashion a makeshift sled with the rope and, after a wild ride marked by screams and shouts, pick themselves up at the bottom of the slope. Amazingly, no one is hurt. They push on.

At seven the next morning, the trio hears sweet music in the distance: a steam whistle calling whalers to work. That afternoon, they reach the whaling station of Stromness and march to the manager's office.

Thoralf Sórlle knows Shackleton well but considers him lost somewhere at the bottom of the Weddell Sea. When he hears a knock at his door, he opens it to find three men in the most ragged clothing imaginable, their long hair matted and stiff, their faces black except for their eyes. Sórlle stares for a long moment.

"Who are you?" he says at last.

The man in the middle steps forward. "My name," he says in a quiet voice, "is Shackleton."

Three-and-a-half months later, after three attempts blocked by the ever-present ice, Shackleton is able to direct a ship to the familiar spit of land on Elephant Island. As they approach, Shackleton sees a group of disheveled men gathering on the beach, waving. A boat is lowered, and an impatient Shackleton climbs in.

Finally, the boat is close enough for Shackleton to be heard. "Are you all well?" he calls.

"All safe, all well" is the reply.

"Thank God!" The relief for Shackleton is indescribable. The grin on his face, however, says it all.

Would You? Could You?

(Share your answers if you're reading in a group)

Early polar exploration was no pleasure cruise for expedition leaders. Those who dared to search for the secrets of earth's ice-laden extremities were more likely to discover dissension, starvation, disease, insanity, and death. Charles F. Hall, captain of the first American attempt to reach the North Pole, was poisoned by his men in 1871. Adolphus Greely lost nineteen of his twenty-five men (including one he had executed) and was accused of cannibalism in the 1880s. Admiral Robert E. Peary's crew accused him of brutality and blamed him for at least one suicide in the 1890s. Robert F. Scott led his party of four to the South Pole, but all starved to death on the return trip in 1912.

Shackleton's expeditions were different. His men respected and almost revered him. They had full confidence in his decisions and ability to lead them out of trouble. Nearly a century later, despite falling short of every goal he originally set, Shackleton is universally admired. But what exactly was the quality of Shackleton's leadership? Does it still exist today? Do *you* have it? If you were in the same circumstances, *could you* have led Shackleton's men out of their incredible predicament on the Weddell Sea?

- How did Shackleton inspire his men to endure and work together? List some examples. Do you see any drawbacks to his approach?

- What are the qualities of great leadership? Which do you have? Which do you lack?

- What kind of leader was Jesus with his disciples? How was Shackleton the same? How was he different?

- Pastor and author Rick Warren has said that integrity and love are the biblical basis for leadership. Do you agree? Was this Shackleton's approach? Do you see evidence of this among our nation's leaders today? How about in your community? At your workplace?

- The Bible tells us that "The husband is the head of the wife as Christ is the head of the church," and "Husbands, love your wives, just as Christ loved the church and gave himself up for her to make her holy" (Eph. 5:23, 25–26). What does this mean to you in terms of leadership within your marriage and family?

- What kind of leader are you at home? Do the principles that Shackleton applied to his men in the Antarctic also apply to your family? If not, what are the most important qualities for leading a family?

- Shackleton later wrote of the *Endurance* expedition, "I have no doubt that Providence guided us, not only across the snow fields, but across the storm-white sea that separated Elephant Island from our landing place on South Georgia. I know that during the long and racking march of thirty-six hours over the unnamed mountains and glaciers of South Georgia, it seemed to me often that we were four, not three." How important do you think this sense of "Providence" was to Shackleton? What does it mean for any leader? Can a leader be effective without God's presence in his life?

Reporting In

Ask the Lord for new insight into what it means to be a leader. Pray that he will show you how to become the leader he designed you to be.

Hitting the Trail

(This is just for you)

Some of us are born leaders. Some of us would rather let others take the point. All of us face times when we are called to lead and when we are expected to submit to another authority. No matter where your comfort zone lies, you can do better.

- Make a list of your leadership roles—father, mother, office manager, Sunday school teacher—whatever they may be. What can you change this week to become more like Shackleton—or, more importantly, like Jesus?

  _____

  _____

  _____

  _____

- Now list your subordinate roles. Are you the kind of team member who helps your leader accomplish goals? Does your leader see you as a valued partner or a mal-

172

content? How would God have us respond to our leaders? (Hint: Read Ephesians 6:5–8.)

_____

_____

_____

- If you aren't already in a position of leadership, volunteer for a task that will give you the opportunity to develop your ability to lead. Keep a journal about your experience, either here or in a notebook.

_____

_____

_____

New Territory

(For those who want to explore further)

Watch the *NOVA* documentary *Shackleton's Voyage of Endurance* or read Alfred Lansing's *Endurance: Shackleton's Incredible Voyage.*

- What impressed you the most about Shackleton's leadership? When did he stumble, and how did he recover?
- Who else emerged as a leader on the expedition? Who displayed less admirable qualities? How would you have fared as a member of Shackleton's crew?

14

Nightmare in Mogadishu

Teach me your way, O LORD;
lead me in a straight path because of my oppressors.

Psalm 27:11

Three military Humvees filled with US Army Rangers move at a steady pace through the narrow, unpaved streets of downtown Mogadishu, Somalia. The sounds of gunfire and explosions are everywhere. It seems as if the entire city is unloading its fury against the small convoy.

Ranger Sergeant Jeff Struecker, sitting in the right front seat, commands the lead vehicle. The twenty-four-year-old from Fort Dodge, Iowa, has already seen combat in Panama and the Persian Gulf, but he's never faced a scene like this. Bullets fill the air, many pinging off the metal exterior of the Humvees.

Private First Class Brad Paulson, from the Midwest, mans the .50-caliber machine gun at the top of the lead Humvee. He's swinging it back and forth, trying to return fire everywhere. "Paulson, just take the left side!" Struecker shouts.

"Pilla, you cover the right!" Sergeant Dominick Pilla is a large kid from New Jersey, known in the Ranger squadron for practical jokes and playing the lead in humorous skits. He's behind a metal bomb protection plate, shooting an M-60 machine gun out a side window.

The October 3, 1993, mission had started well. Task Force Rangers had been in Mogadishu for nearly two months as part of a United Nations effort to capture a warlord named Mohamed Farrah Aidid. The country was in chaos, ripped apart by competing factions. Aidid, who controlled the drug trade and food supplies, was the most powerful of the warlords.

In the past few weeks, the Ranger force had conducted six raids into the city, each time capturing one of Aidid's important associates. This time, an informant identified two targets meeting in the same location. It was a great opportunity. The drawback? It was downtown, a block north of the Olympic Hotel—right in the middle of Aidid's territory.

That afternoon eight Black Hawk helicopters and other gunships swooped in, dropping Delta Force operators (D-boys) and Rangers into the city. Struecker, meanwhile, had led a convoy of Humvees into the city. Once the D-boys secured the targets, the convoy's task was to transport the prisoners three miles back to the Ranger base. The whole operation involved 160 soldiers and was expected to take thirty minutes.

Everything seemed to go smoothly at the target house. The bad guys had been rounded up and were nearly ready for transport. Then Struecker got the word: the Rangers had a casualty. Private First Class Todd Blackburn, fresh out of a Florida high school and new to Mogadishu, had missed the rope coming out of a Black Hawk. He'd fallen seventy feet and was severely injured and unconscious. Struecker was ordered to load Blackburn onto a backboard and into a cargo Humvee, then take two more Humvees and return to base.

Struecker instructed Private First Class Jeremy Kerr, his driver, to move at a deliberate pace. "We need to take it slow, so we don't break Blackburn's neck," he said. "Dodge every pothole you can." But the enemy fire was intense. At some points they had to blast through makeshift barricades.

Now they have covered five blocks and are making the final turn onto a boulevard that will lead them out of the slums and back "home." As they turn, Pilla spots a gunman pointing an AK-47 at him. Pilla quickly aims. Both men fire at virtually the same moment.

Struecker hears Specialist Tim Moynihan screaming, "Pilla's hit! He's shot in the head!"

Struecker glances back. Pilla is slumped into Moynihan's lap. Blood is everywhere.

"What do we do? Dom's killed!" Moynihan yells. Kerr and Paulson begin talking excitedly as well.

Struecker senses the situation getting out of control. For a moment, he starts to panic himself. A good soldier and friend, a man he is responsible for, is dead. He swallows. But then he realizes he needs to put all that out of his mind. *Take charge, Jeff*, he thinks.

"Moynihan," he says. "Stop what you're doing. Take your weapon and face right; pick up Dominick's sector of fire. Kerr, step on it! Fly down this road as fast as you can!" It was time to forget worrying about a bumpy ride making Blackburn's injury worse. They needed to concentrate on getting out of there.

A few minutes later, the three Humvees roar through the gate to the Ranger base. A medical team approaches and begins pulling Pilla's body out of the back of the vehicle.

"Just leave him alone," Struecker says. "He's gone. Go to the other vehicle. Blackburn's over there."

Struecker can't believe what just happened. Pilla is the first Ranger casualty in Mogadishu. The sergeant walks away from the Humvee, takes off his helmet, and hurls it against a stack of sandbags. *God, like, so what's the deal here? How come this all fell apart on me?*

He turns and realizes the remainder of his squad is staring at him. They've never seen him lose control before.

A lieutenant approaches. His face is pale. Slowly, he says, "Another Black Hawk has gone down. You need to get your squad ready to go back in. We need to get to the crash site."

"What do you mean, *another*?" Struecker learns that Aidid's militia has taken down two helicopters in the city with RPGs (rocket propelled grenades). No one knows how many Rangers survived the crashes, and Aidid's men are closing in quickly.

Oh no, Struecker thinks. They've already lost one man; the rest of his team barely escaped. Now they're being ordered to revisit a nightmare. Yet Struecker knows that now more than ever, he can't let his men see his concern.

"Sergeant Mitchell!" he says. "Get your vehicle down to the supply point and get more ammo! Get some for us too, while you're at it. And don't forget to fuel up.

"Moynihan! Thomas! Go get some water, and make sure there's nothing in the vehicles that's not absolutely mission-essential! Get some night vision goggles too. This might take a while." The men hesitate for a moment, then move into action.

A Delta Force operator walks over. "Sergeant, you don't want to take your men back out in all that blood. You need to clean up your vehicle first."

Struecker glances at the Humvee and the evidence of Pilla's grisly death. He realizes the operator is right—his men are psyched out enough. "Roger that," he says.

He turns to Kerr and Paulson, both probably nineteen years old. He can see in their eyes that they're overwhelmed. How can he order them to take on this job?

"Men," Struecker says, "I could use some help cleaning up this vehicle—but I'm not going to make you do it. If you want to volunteer, okay. But if you'd rather not, I understand. Just go help load up more fuel and ammo instead."

Both privates stay with Struecker as he drives the Humvee to a water tanker. Using a sponge, a yellow brush, buckets of water, and their bare hands, the men go to work. Pilla's ammo can is still in the Humvee, filled with blood and unused bullets. *Man, we're gonna need this*, Struecker thinks. He pulls out the ammo and dumps it in a bucket of clean water.

The radio is broadcasting news from the fight in Mogadishu. Most of it isn't good. By the sound of the reports, Struecker estimates there may be up to ten thousand Somalis battling the small Ranger force. He finally tells Kerr to turn the radio off.

I'm going to die tonight, Struecker thinks. *And what's just as bad, I'm going to get every one of my men killed. I just know it. There's no way we can survive another run back into that city. Tomorrow this squad is going to have ten dead Rangers instead of just one.*

Struecker's thoughts shift to his pregnant wife, Dawn, back at the Ranger base at Fort Benning, Georgia. *My child is never going to know his daddy. This is it, tonight. How is she going to manage having a baby and raising it all by herself?*

He begins to pray silently. *God, I'm in deep trouble, as you can see. I need help. I'm not saying you should get me out of this. I just need your help.*

His mind returns to the Rangers in his charge. *God, please don't let me do anything stupid that puts the rest of my men into a slaughter tonight. If any of them get killed, I sure don't want it to be my fault.* Struecker doesn't hear a response to his prayer, at least not in words. Yet he's pleased to discover a renewed sense of peace.

He inspects the cleaned-out Humvee. "Men, we're good. Let's load up and get ready to move."

Specialist Brad Thomas got married a few months ago. He'd been on the beach with Pilla earlier in the day. When the Humvees pulled into the base with Pilla's splattered remains, Thomas was crying. Now he approaches Struecker.

"Sergeant, you know I *really* don't want to go back out," he says.

Struecker isn't surprised by Thomas's statement. There will be serious consequences for any Ranger who asks out of a mission. But Thomas is expressing what everyone is thinking.

Struecker feels eyes on him, watching to see how he'll react. He could end the specialist's career right here. He tries a different approach.

"Listen," he says in a low voice. "I understand how you feel. I'm married too. Don't think of yourself as a coward. I know you're scared. I've never been in a situation quite like this either. But we've got to go. It's our job. The difference between being a coward and being a hero is not whether you're scared or not. It's what you do while you're scared."

Thomas walks away, and Struecker mounts his Humvee. A minute later, Struecker glances into his rearview mirror. He sees Thomas climbing aboard one of the other Humvees. The convoy is ready to go.

Struecker and his men lead the way back into the city, where they survive withering fire and an RPG that skips across the hood of their Humvee. They encounter the remains of the original convoy, which had been searching for the first downed Black Hawk and is now shot to pieces. The mission changes for Struecker and his convoy; they're ordered to transport the wounded from the original convoy back to base.

At 11:30 that night, Struecker's Humvee leads a convoy into the city for the third time. Rangers from the downed Black Hawks and early rescue attempts are still in Mogadishu. Some are dead, but the Ranger motto is "leave no man behind"—dead or alive. Struecker's Humvee is the first vehicle in and, after one of the longest nights anyone can remember, the very last to leave.

On the way out, while still taking fire from the enemy, Paulson yells from his position atop the Humvee, "Sergeant! We've got bodies chasing after us from down the street."

"Open fire," Struecker says.

"Sergeant, I think these are our guys!"

Struecker turns to look. He can't believe it. About a dozen Rangers are running in their direction. Somehow they hadn't been picked up. He can see the terror in their eyes.

The rest of the convoy moves on, but Struecker's Humvee and another turn back. In the midst of some of the heaviest fire of the mission, they quickly round up the remaining Rangers and finally, mercifully, return to base. Behind them, the streets are virtually covered by thousands of empty brass shell casings. They glisten in the morning sunlight.

Would You? Could You?

(Share your answers if you're reading in a group)
There's nothing that twists your gut quite like the knowledge that you're going into a hairy situation with an excellent chance of not coming back out. The members of the United Nations force in Somalia in October 1993 faced exactly that feeling. Eighteen US soldiers died and another seventy-three were injured during the battle in Mogadishu. In Sergeant Jeff Struecker's squad, Brad Paulson and another gunner were wounded. Dominick Pilla was the lone death. Struecker was awarded a Bronze Star for Valor for his service.

The men in Struecker's squad came to know that gut-twisting particularly well. After the first raid, they knew what they were up against in downtown Mogadishu. It was far more intense than anything they'd encountered before. When the order came to go back—and later, to go back again—they had to confront their fear and mortality. Struecker had an additional burden. He not only had to face down his own frustration and fear but also inspire the remaining eight Rangers in his squad, as well as others recruited to join the new convoys.

Leadership styles are as varied as the men and women who lead. Some rule with an iron fist. Some employ encouragement. Others lead by example. Many attempt a combination of these and other techniques. Whatever the method, we all know the value of strong leadership, especially during times of crisis. How do *you* respond to a crisis? If you were Jeff Struecker in October 1993, how would you have fared as the bullets blazed during the battle in Mogadishu?

- Have you ever had to lead others in a life-or-death situation? How did you handle it? Does having that extra responsibility make it harder or easier to function during a crisis?

- On two occasions during the Mogadishu conflict—when Pilla's blood had to be cleaned up and when Thomas confronted him—Sergeant Struecker gave his men a choice instead of an order. Was it the right strategy? How could it have backfired?

- After Jesus Christ washed the feet of his disciples, he said, "I have set you an example that you should do as I have done for you. I tell you the truth, no servant is greater than his master, nor is a messenger greater than the one who sent him" (John 13:15–16). How did Struecker demonstrate this kind of servant leadership when he joined his men in cleaning the Humvee? What did it say to his men? Was it worth the time he could have spent preparing for the upcoming mission?

- As a Ranger, Struecker was trained to not show fear in front of his men. Today, however, he advocates an approach that combines toughness, control, and honesty: "I've learned that subordinates relate much better to me when I'm not trying to be so stoic. They appreciate knowing that I have to deal with fear just as they do." Do you agree with that approach? Why or why not? How does it compare to how you lead your family or co-workers?

- As a born-again Christian (and now a US Army chaplain), Jeff Struecker has endured the taunts and behind-the-back comments of fellow soldiers who don't understand his faith. How does being a Christian affect one's ability to lead non-Christians? What are the obstacles? What are the advantages?

Reporting In

When was the last time you provided an example of servant leadership? If you can't remember, maybe it's time to ask the

Lord to send you an opportunity. While you're at it, ask him how you're doing as a leader and ambassador for him.

Hitting the Trail

(This is just for you)

Leadership is a tricky business. Jeff Struecker has advocated toughness, control, and honesty—yet in Mogadishu, he at times demonstrated compassion (to Brad Thomas) and frustration (when he threw his helmet), and he kept his fears to himself. Finding the right approach for each situation may be the greatest leadership challenge of all.

- Who are the leaders in your life who most inspire you? Why do you admire and respect them? Write down their names and what it is about them and their approach that moves you. Is Christ on your list? Why or why not?

  _____

  _____

  _____

  _____

- Think about the people you are called on to lead. What leadership style do they respond to best? Write down your answers. How are you at delivering that style? Write that down too.

  _____

  _____

  _____

  _____

- Here's the big one—what can you do in the next week to improve your leadership technique? Do you need to work on being tougher, more in control, or more open and honest? Record your thoughts here.

_____

_____

_____

New Territory

(For those who want to explore further)

Read Mark Bowden's bestseller *Black Hawk Down* or Jeff Struecker's *The Road to Unafraid*. If you don't mind some grisly scenes, watch the Columbia Pictures movie *Black Hawk Down*.

- There were many tests of leadership throughout the conflict in Somalia in 1993. Who do you feel passed the test? Who failed? If some of the decisions had changed, how might things have turned out differently?
- Is there a conflict between the life of a soldier and the calling of a Christian? Is there such a thing as a "just" war? Was the United Nations intervention in Somalia such a war? What do you base your answers on?

15

Death Trap

When a man becomes a fireman his greatest act of bravery has been accomplished. What
he does after that is all in the line of work.

Edward F. Croker

Robert Wagner "Wag" Dodge bends one arm and grimaces. He's just jumped out of a C-47 and parachuted
onto a remote, rocky slope in Montana wilderness.
The landing was less than perfect; his arm has a puncture
wound. "My elbow," he says, "aches like blazes."

For the thirty-three-year-old Dodge, a nine-year veteran
of the US Forest Service—including the last four as a smoke-
jumper foreman—the statement is practically a speech. He's
a quiet man by nature, with a fondness for poetry. He's so
quiet that years later his wife says, "I loved him very much,
but I didn't know him very well."

His fourteen-man crew doesn't know him well either. None
have served on a fire with him before. Dodge realizes it's a young
team. A few hours before, Eldon Diettert was called away from

185

a luncheon in honor of his nineteenth birthday. Walter Rumsey, from Kansas, is twenty-one. Robert Sallee lied about his age to land this job; he's just seventeen. For many of the crew, including Rumsey and Sallee, this is their first jump into a real fire.

The fire itself, ignited by lightning, has consumed about sixty acres. It's burning along the south rim of a place called Mann Gulch. It's August 5, 1949.

By 4:10 p.m., all of Dodge's crew has parachuted to the ground along with tools and overnight gear, which are scattered over the hillside. He signals the plane that everyone is accounted for. It takes until nearly 5 p.m. to gather everything in one place. All is intact except one piece of equipment—the parachute for the radio never opened.

From the landing site, Rumsey can see the flank of the fire, roughly fifteen hundred yards to the south. It doesn't look particularly impressive, though because of the steep and rocky ground, he expects it will be a chore to finish it off.

The crew hears a shout from the fire area. Dodge orders his second-in-command, twenty-four-year-old Bill Hellman, to make sure the crew gets something to eat while he walks over to find out who's fighting the fire. It turns out to be one man, Jim Harrison, a recreation and fire prevention guard who'd first spotted the fire from his station to the south.

When Dodge examines the fire, he isn't thrilled by what he sees. The heat is intense, preventing him from moving closer than one hundred feet. Worse, the fire is threatening a thick area of second-generation Douglas fir and ponderosa pine.

Dodge and Harrison quickly rejoin the rest of the smoke jumpers. "Let's get away from this thick reproduction," Dodge says. "It's a death trap. It'll be safer to work the lower side of the fire. Me and Harrison here are going back to the gear to get some grub. The rest of you cross to the other side of the gulch and start heading down to the river so you can work the fire from behind the wind. But don't go straight down the gulley. Angle up a bit and follow the contour of the slope so you can keep an eye on the flames."

As the crew ambles toward the Missouri River, Rumsey notices that the fire is burning with more intensity. He thinks it "a very interesting spectacle." A few of the men pause to take photos.

As Dodge eats with Harrison, he also keeps an eye on the fire. He too sees it starting to boil up and grows more concerned. He grabs a can of Irish white potatoes and, along with Harrison, catches back up with the crew, where he organizes them into a line with himself in the lead and Hellman at the back. They begin walking toward the river into a headwind of twenty to thirty miles an hour.

It is 5:40 p.m.

Over the next five minutes, Dodge leads his young crew through scattered timber four hundred yards down the gulch. Once they reach the river, they can attack the fire from that side, and they'll have a safe area for escape if needed. They have about a thousand yards to go.

There are two prevalent theories on what happens next in Mann Gulch. One is that downdrafts from a small local thunderstorm blow from the south rim into the mouth of the gulch. The other is that wind, high temperatures, and the shape of the canyon combine to create whirlwinds that move to the north. Either of these, or a combination of both, could easily loft firebrands from the south rim fire into Mann Gulch.

At 5:45 p.m., Wag Dodge isn't thinking about theories. He's concerned and walking quickly. He crests a rise and suddenly stops short.

Unmistakable bursts of orange ignite the tops of the trees ahead, already exploding into larger swaths of flame. The fire has jumped in front of them. It's coming after them.

Dodge figures they are two hundred yards, maybe less, from the advancing fire. He orders his crew to turn around.

Sallee and Rumsey are at the rear of the column because they each carry unsheathed, two-man handsaws. They can't see the fire ahead, but they are alarmed at the sudden shift in the crew's direction. As the line reassembles, the two rookies hurry to the front, right behind Dodge. One man still seems unconcerned; Dave Navon stops to snap a couple more photos before turning to follow the rest.

The crown fire is probably advancing through the treetops at a speed of about 120 feet per minute. Dodge doesn't think they have time to cut at a right angle up the steep and rocky grade to the north rim. For the next 450 yards, they march quickly back the way they came, up the more gradual grade of the gulch's north slope. Some of the men begin to jog.

At 5:53 p.m., Dodge turns to look. The fire is gaining on them, now a hundred yards back or less. He realizes they are in a deadly race. He orders the men to throw down their packs and heavy tools. Some have already done so. Some are so focused on escape that they ignore Dodge's instruction. Diettert continues carrying his shovel until Rumsey catches up with him, takes it away, and leans it against a tree.

The fire grows in strength and speed. There's no longer doubt about the desperation of the moment. Hearts pound. Throats burn. The fire's roar is deafening, like a jet taking off. It feels as if it's pulling ahead of them on each side. The temperature is searing, far above one hundred degrees Fahrenheit. Within the fire's core, temperatures may be as high as 1,800 degrees.

The men literally run for their lives. Adrenaline is pushing them to move faster than they would have thought possible, but even so there are limits. Exhaustion catches up first with Harrison, who unlike the rest has been battling the blaze for four hours. He sits down, a heavy pack on his back, and makes no effort to take it off. No one stops to encourage him on.

Rumsey has one thought steamrolling through his brain: *The top of the ridge. The top of the ridge.* There's too much smoke now to see it. But he knows it's there.

The landscape changes as the crew charges uphill. The trees are fewer; the men are running mostly through tall, dry grass. Suddenly they break out into an open area of cheatgrass and fescue. It's a tinderbox. Here, with the wind behind it and no trees to slow it, the fire may race at six hundred feet per minute.

For the first time, in brief clearings through the smoke, the men make out the ridge at the top of the gulch, perhaps two hundred yards away. Everyone is focused on the ridge.

Everyone except Dodge. He knows the fire will keep gaining speed. It's now just fifty yards away. He figures they have about thirty seconds. They aren't going to make it.

Dodge's next act is inspiration born of desperation. He's never been taught to do this, never even thought about it before. Suddenly he just knows it's the logical thing to do. He stops running, snatches a book of matches from his pocket, and bends over to light a fire.

Rumsey sprints past Dodge, thinking, *That's a very good idea*, though he's not sure why it's good. He keeps aiming for the ridge.

Sallee, running with Rumsey, has a different reaction: *He's lost it. He's gone nuts.*

Dodge's fire burns rapidly and at a right angle, toward the north rim. In seconds, one hundred square feet of earth is scorched black.

A few of the men are already past Dodge, but more, perhaps as many as eight, are close. "This way!" Dodge yells. "This way!"

Some of the men slow down or stop. Some, if not all of them, probably can't hear him over the crackle and roar of the inferno. Dodge's fire makes no sense to them. A voice emerges from the smoke: "To heck with that, I'm getting out of here." The men keep running.

Rumsey and Sallee, with Diettert right behind them, angle up the east side of Dodge's fire toward a reef about thirty yards below the north rim. It's a wall of rimrock twelve to twenty feet high. They have seconds to find a way through.

Please God, I'm not ready to die, Sallee prays. In the next instant, running alongside Dodge's fire, he thinks, *Dodge is trying to burn me to death.*

The smoke clears briefly, long enough for Rumsey to make out a crevice in the rimrock. Every instinct is pushing him toward that hole. Nothing else matters.

He's there. He stumbles in and collapses. Sallee is right behind him. He glares at Rumsey, who scrambles up and through the opening.

Sallee turns for a last look down the slope. He sees Dodge jump over the flames at the edge of his fire, into the blackness. Dodge waves his arms and appears to shout at four or five men who are twenty to fifty feet away. Sallee finally understands. Dodge wants the men to join him on the black ground. It's a safety zone.

Sallee turns back and follows Rumsey through the crevice.

Dodge keeps hollering, but no one stops to figure out what's he's saying. He pours water from his canteen onto a handkerchief, jams it against his mouth, and dives into the scorched dirt. Seconds later, the main fire, with a front up to three hundred feet long, hits. The winds inside it are so powerful that Dodge's body is lifted into the air three separate times. Yet because of a thin layer of oxygen along the ground, he survives.

Rumsey and Sallee break through the rimrock and over the ridge. There's fire here too, but also a large rockslide. They move into the middle of the rocks. Sallee still has his felt hat and canteen. He pours water into the hat and pushes it against his face. The fire rages around them, but both of the rookies also survive.

None of the other smoke jumpers are as fortunate. Two are badly burned and die the next day. Rescuers find four charred bodies near the top of the ridge, far beyond Dodge's fire. One is found near the bottom of the slope. This smoke jumper apparently fell, broke his leg, and rolled into the fire. Harrison's body is among those closer to the bottom. The hands on his wristwatch are melted to the time of 5:56 p.m. The rest of the bodies are scattered along the north slope, their faces pointed upward, as if still fighting to reach the ridge.

Among them is Eldon Diettert, the birthday boy, whose remains are found against the rimrock about a hundred yards north of Rumsey and Sallee's crevice. No one knows why he didn't follow them into the opening. Did the smoke blind him? Was there something about that spot he didn't like? The answer is lost to those left behind. It is part of the enduring mystery and tragedy that is the story of Mann Gulch.

Would You? Could You?

(Share your answers if you're reading in a group)

To this day, the 1949 Mann Gulch fire remains a topic of tragedy and controversy. Thirteen men died during the blowup. Only Colorado's 1994 Storm King Mountain fire has claimed the lives of more smoke jumpers (fourteen). After Mann Gulch, some parents of the dead sued the Forest Service, alleging carelessness and poor decision making. In more recent years, particularly following the publication of Norman Maclean's bestseller *Young Men and Fire*, the Forest Service has been accused of "scattering" elements of the story immediately after the fire and of doctoring the testimony of a survivor.

Wag Dodge's performance in Mann Gulch is fascinating. During what was expected to be a routine assignment, he unwittingly led his men into disaster and then attempted to lead them back out of it. Under intense pressure, he also had the imagination to invent an escape plan that is standard education for today's firefighters.

What kind of leader was Dodge? Courageous? Irresponsible? Creative? How would *you* perform with flames bearing down and lives on the line?

- What kind of leader are you in a crisis? *Would you* be able to come up with an innovative solution when every second counts? *Could you* inspire others to try an untested idea when their lives depend on it?

- In the late 1940s, the Forest Service required all crew members and "overhead" (foremen, squad leaders, and spotters) to take a three-week course together at the beginning of each fire season. Part of the goal was to establish familiarity between crews and their bosses, since shifts rotated constantly. Dodge, however, was in charge of base maintenance and missed this course. Did his lack of familiarity with his men—and theirs with him—contribute to their ignoring him in the moment of crisis? Are you more likely to trust a boss you know?

- Dodge was quiet by nature. Walter Rumsey later said, "Dodge has a characteristic in him. It is hard to tell what he is thinking." Should he have communicated more of his thoughts and concerns to the crew? How much should a leader say about doubts to his team? Is the answer different when time is critical?

- Dodge originally argued against the smoke jumpers' landing site because it was too steep for a helicopter to land if any of his crew were injured. It was the spotter's call, however, and Dodge finally accepted the decision. Should he have been more forceful in objecting? How does someone balance the safety of their crew against the hazards of an inherently dangerous job?

- Expecting to be on the ground through the night, Dodge took time to eat with Harrison and allowed his men to proceed down the gulch without him. Given the conditions, was it a mistake? How important is it for leaders to have a thick skin, knowing they will be second-guessed?

- Although Native Americans lit escape fires on the prairie a century before, it appears neither Dodge nor any of his men had prior knowledge of the technique in Mann Gulch. How important is flexibility and creativity to good leadership?

- Think about some of the Bible's most important leaders: Moses, David, Peter, Paul, and of course, Jesus. What were their strengths? What were their weaknesses? How would they have performed in Wag Dodge's shoes?

Reporting In

Someday, somewhere, you will be called upon to make life-altering decisions in an instant. Pray now for the Lord's guidance and wisdom for that moment.

Hitting the Trail

(This is just for you)

Wag Dodge put on his gear and got into an airplane three times after the Mann Gulch fire. Each time, he couldn't bring himself to jump. His smoke-jumping days were over. The emotional toll on leaders can be a heavy one, especially when things go wrong. How are you suited or not suited to be a leader?

- List examples from your present or past when you have been in a position of authority. What did you do right? What do you wish you'd done better?

  _____

  _____

  _____

- Read about the life of Moses starting in the second chapter of Exodus. How did his leadership compare to that of secular leaders today? How does it compare to yours?

  _____

  _____

  _____

- What leadership role do you wish you could take on in the future? Record here the steps that would be needed to make it happen. Ask the Lord if he wants you to move in this direction.

_____

_____

_____

New Territory

(For those who want to explore further)

Read Norman Maclean's *Young Men and Fire*, the story of the Mann Gulch fire, and *Fire on the Mountain*, John Maclean's account of the 1994 fire on Colorado's Storm King Mountain.

- How were these two tragedies comparable? How were they different?
- Do you have what it takes to be a smoke jumper?

16

Love and Death in the Andes

These three remain: faith, hope and love.
But the greatest of these is love.

1 Corinthians 13:13

Think fast, Nando!"
Twenty-two-year-old Nando Parrado turns just in time to catch a rugby ball hurled his way. He's standing in an airplane full of young people, members of a rugby team from Uruguay. Nando smiles, passes the ball on, and sits down. Everyone on the Fairchild turboprop is talking and laughing. They are on their way to Chile for an exhibition match and are determined to enjoy the trip. It is Friday, October 13, 1971.

For Nando, it is another carefree moment in an untroubled life. The son of a prosperous hardware store owner, he lives in the moment. He enjoys rugby, fast cars, and chasing girls, though he is shy and gangly and not nearly as successful with women as his teammate and best friend, Panchito Abal.

He's sitting next to Panchito now. Moments before, his friend asked to switch seats in hopes of glimpsing the majestic mountains through the clouds below. They are flying through the Andes, one of the most beautiful and formidable mountain ranges on earth. Aconcagua, the highest peak in the Western Hemisphere, stands at nearly twenty-three thousand feet.

"Fasten your seat belts, please," the flight steward says. "There is going to be some turbulence ahead."

Suddenly, the plane drops several hundred feet and bounces four times, as if driving over speed bumps. Some of the players shout, "Ole!" Nando looks across the aisle, where his mother and twenty-year-old sister, Susy, are sitting. He's invited them to join him on this holiday.

Nando sees that his mother, holding Susy's hand, is worried. He smiles to reassure her.

Once again, violent air currents force the plane down several hundred feet. Nando's stomach lurches.

Panchito, at the window, elbows Nando. "Look at this, Nando," he says. "Should we be so close to the mountains?"

Nando looks. Through clear spots in the clouds, he sees rock and snow—not far below where they ought to be, but only twenty-five feet from the bobbing tip of the plane's wing.

The Fairchild's engines whine as they strain to climb higher. Nando's mother and sister turn toward Nando, eyes wide with fright.

The plane shudders violently, accompanied by the screams of metal and men. Nando sees open sky where the Fairchild's ceiling should be. Cold air slashes his face. Clouds swirl around him. Then he is thrown forward into blackness.

"Nando, can you hear me? Are you okay?"

The shadow above him is a person, Nando realizes. It has dark hair and brown eyes. Nando tries to answer, but no words come.

He is cold. His head hurts. He loses his focus on the shadow and fades back into a strange and disturbing dreamworld.

Soon, however, the dream fades. He awakens to a nightmare.

Nando is lying within the broken fuselage of the Fairchild. He has a serious wound in his head. He has been in a coma for three days. The plane has crashed in the snow on a glacier somewhere high in the Andes. His mother and Panchito are dead. So are the crew, save for the delirious mechanic. Of the forty-five people who boarded the chartered plane, fifteen are gone. Several more, including Nando's sister, are alive but badly injured.

The survivors are shaken, but they have not given up. In the first moments after the crash, Roberto Canessa and Gustavo Zerbino, rugby players who were also medical students, cared as best they could for the injured. As always, team captain Marcelo Perez took charge. Marcelo led those healthy enough to free passengers trapped beneath crumpled seats. He also organized a crew to bury the dead in the snow and build a sheltering wall to help block the night's subzero temperatures.

Marcelo leads the group in other ways. He rations the meager food supply—a scrap of chocolate, a capful of wine, and a teaspoonful of jam or canned fish is the daily portion. He sleeps in the coldest section of the cramped fuselage and insists that the other healthy survivors join him. He gives everyone tasks to keep their minds away from terror. Most importantly, he parcels out hope, repeating that search parties are on the way.

Nando, however, is not so certain rescuers will discover the Fairchild in this vast desert of snow in the clouds. *No one will find us*, a voice inside his head whispers. *We will die here. We must make a plan. We must save ourselves.*

On their eighth day on the mountain, Nando's despair sinks further when Susy, his baby sister, dies as he lies next to her, his arms around her. He is overwhelmed with grief and rage. Yet when he remembers his love for his father back in Uruguay and the suffering he must also be enduring, he calms. *I will come home*, Nando vows. *I will not let the bond between us be broken. I promise you, I will not die here!*

On the tenth day, the twenty-seven remaining survivors discuss another crisis—they are starving to death. What little food that could be scrounged from the broken remains of the Fairchild is nearly gone. Nothing grows on the glacier. There is only rock and snow. Everyone is becoming weak and lethargic.

Roberto Canessa brings into the open what several have already whispered about. "Our bodies are consuming themselves," he says. "Unless we eat some protein soon, we will die, and the only protein here is in the bodies of our friends."

Shock and silence are the first reactions. A debate ensues.

"But what will this do to our souls?" someone asks. "Could God forgive such a thing?"

"If you don't eat, you are choosing to die," Roberto says. "Would God forgive that? I believe God wants us to do whatever we can to survive."

In the end, Roberto and three others trek with shards of glass to the corpses buried in the snow. They return with thin strips of flesh. Many, though not all, accept and force down the meat. Nando is among them. He feels no shame or guilt. Instead, he realizes it kindles a trace of hope. They have found the courage to fight back against the unseen enemy that is trying to kill them.

The next day, eighteen-year-old Roy Harley is outside the fuselage, holding a small transistor radio to his ear. He has constructed a crude antenna from electrical wires found in the Fairchild. The signal is weak and frequently interrupted by static, but he makes out the voice of a newscaster.

Suddenly Roy begins to sob. "They have canceled the search!" he shouts. "They are abandoning us!"

Marcelo, who was helping Roy with the antenna, drops to his knees and howls in anguish. For the brave captain, it is a blow he cannot recover from. He has stayed strong and rallied them all, but his hopes were pinned on rescue. His confidence and optimism are shattered. He slips into despair.

In his place, a team of leaders emerges to inspire the survivors. Among these are three cousins: Fito Strauch, Eduardo Strauch, and Daniel Fernandez. Another is Nando, who begins talking forcefully about climbing out of their mountainous trap before they are too weak. The others soon agree.

Nando doesn't feel like a leader. He has always been one to follow others. He is confused and scared, and has little faith in his plan. But he is desperate to leave this place so full of death.

It is October 29. The survivors remain frightened, but they have a plan. Nando and three others have been designated as "expeditionaries." They are preparing to escape, gathering what little supplies and clothes they can muster. The plan lifts the spirits of the group. Perhaps the worst is over. Perhaps they will recover from this nightmare.

That evening, Nando is lying next to Liliana and Javier Methol on the floor of the fuselage. Javier is a cousin of Panchito. The Methols, in their thirties, are the oldest of the survivors.

Nando confesses doubts about his faith to Liliana.

"God has saved us so far," Liliana says. "We must trust him."

"But why would God save us and let the others die?" Nando asks. "My mother, my sister, Panchito, Guido? Didn't they want God to save them?"

"There is no way to understand God or his logic."

"Then why should we trust him? What about all the Jews who died in concentration camps? What about all the innocents killed in plagues and purges and natural disasters? Why would he turn his back on them but still find time for us?"

199

Liliana sighs. "You are getting too complicated," she says in a kind tone. "All we can do is love God and love others and trust in God's will."

Nando is unconvinced, yet comforted. He drifts into a cold slumber.

He is awakened by something heavy on his chest and ice on his face. In a moment, he realizes what's happened: an avalanche has struck the fuselage and filled it with snow.

Nando tries to move, but he cannot. The snow is already compacting and freezing above him. He is suffocating.

This is my death, he thinks. *Now I will see what lies on the other side.*

Then something rips the snow away from his face. He can breathe again. "Who is it?" a voice shouts.

"Me," he gasps. "It's Nando."

More shouts and sobs follow. People are digging frantically.

In just a few minutes, all is silent. Nando and the rest stare at each other in shock and disbelief. Eight more friends are dead, including Marcelo and Liliana. The mountains are fighting back.

"Nando, are you ready?"

The voice belongs to Roberto Canessa. It is December 12. At last, after blizzards foiled previous expeditions to the east, a team is ready to climb west, toward Chile. The marchers are Nando, Roberto, and "Tintin" Vizintin. The survivors are down to sixteen now—three more have died from injury or starvation.

Nando glances at the snow graves of his friends, then turns to one of the boys. "If you run out of food," he says quietly, "I want you to use my mother and Susy." Then he waves to the rail-thin but still living forms at the Fairchild, turns, and on snowshoes fashioned from seat cushions, starts to walk.

Climbing to a peak near seventeen thousand feet would be a significant challenge for experienced mountaineers equipped with the latest gear. For three weak young men with no gear at all, every step is an invitation to die. Yet they battle on against the ever-steepening slope. Twice, they are forced to camp overnight beneath a rock, lying almost vertical together in their makeshift sleeping bag. Once, Tintin stops climbing in a panic. He can't find anything to grip, and his backpack is too heavy. It's pulling him off the mountain. If he falls, nothing can save him.

"Take off your backpack!" Roberto shouts. "Give it to me!"

Slowly, while concentrating to keep his balance, Tintin slips the pack off his shoulders. Fatigued and frightened, he is able to continue.

On the fourth day, as always, Nando is leading. He has been deceived many times by outcroppings that appear to be the summit, when in fact they only shield his vision of another peak. He ascends a new ridgeline and finds himself on a flat rock about twelve feet in diameter. There is nowhere else to climb. He is at the top.

The view is spectacular—and crushing. Instead of the green valleys he'd hoped to see to the west, there are only more snowcapped mountains. Nando falls to his knees, certain now that he will perish, understanding that life is a fragile dream and death is the only constant. Yet even in his despair, love for his father rises in his heart, pushing out the fear and certainty of death.

The opposite of death is love, Nando thinks. *Only love can turn mere life into a miracle and draw precious meaning from suffering and fear.* He pulls lipstick and a paper bag from his backpack, scrawls "Mt. Seler"—his father's name—on the bag, and shoves it under a rock.

This mountain was my enemy, and now I give it to my father. Whatever happens, at least I have this as my revenge.

The climbers spend another night near the peak and decide that Nando and Roberto will continue on with Tintin's food while he returns to the Fairchild. At the summit the next morning, Nando says, "We may be walking to our deaths, but I would rather walk to meet my death than wait for it to come to me."

"You and I are friends, Nando," Roberto says. "We have been through so much. Now let's go die together."

Somehow the pair stumbles down the mountain without injury. By December 18, the seventh day of their journey, the snow is giving way to patches of ice and loose rock. They discover a wall of ice melting into a flowing stream. It is the beginning of a river. They decide to follow it.

The next day, the sole of Nando's right boot flaps as he walks. It is coming apart. But they are entering a valley. For the first time in more than two months, they see the color green, the sign of living things. Soon they are among plants and trees. Nando refuses, however, to get his hopes up.

Another day passes. Roberto is plagued by a terrible case of diarrhea. He limps with Nando to a plateau overlooking a meadow and the stone walls of a farmer's corral. Inside are cows but also another river that connects with the one they've followed, cutting off their path.

At twilight, both friends are incredibly exhausted and hungry. They are so close, but Roberto especially is at the end of his strength.

Suddenly, Roberto exclaims loudly, "Nando, I see a man!"

Nando, who is nearsighted, squints in the direction Roberto points. "I can't see anything."

"Go! Run!" Roberto shouts. "Go down to the river!"

Nando runs but still sees nothing. Roberto limps down to join him. They give up and are turning back when Nando hears a voice above the rush of the river. He spots a man on horseback on the other bank. The man shouts something, then turns and rides away.

"Did you hear him?" Roberto asks. "What did he say?"

"I only heard one word," Nando replies. "I heard him say 'tomorrow.'"

Roberto looks at Nando, his face a mixture of triumph, torture, and relief.

"We are saved."

Two days later, Nando is in a hospital in San Fernando, Chile. All fifteen of his comrades are alive and being rescued. They have made it.

Nando is alone in his room, amazed to be wearing a clean gown and lying in a clean bed, when he hears a disturbance in the hospital hallway. It is his older sister, Graciela, and her husband. Nando moves to greet them, and Graciela sobs as they embrace. Then Nando sees, at the end of the hallway, a slight man in tears. Nando goes to him and holds him tight, raising him off the floor.

"You see, Papa," he whispers. "I am still strong enough to lift you."

Both, in fact, are being lifted by a love that will never end. For Nando and his family, it is all that matters.

Would You? Could You?

(Share your answers if you're reading in a group)

Of all the survivors of the airplane crash in the Andes, the experience may have changed Nando Parrado the most. Once a somewhat timid and uncertain youth, Nando eventually emerged in the mountains as a courageous leader determined to either reach civilization or die trying. The strength of teammate Marcelo Perez, meanwhile, inspired the group in its first days after the crash, yet Marcelo's fortitude ended when hopes for rescue were lost.

Both of these young men gave the group what was needed when it was needed most: hope and a plan. The crisis in the Andes exposed some of their greatest strengths and weaknesses. What are your strengths and weaknesses as a leader? Would they change when the stakes are life and death? How would you perform in an environment that seems designed to kill you?

- If you were stranded in the Andes, *could you* organize and rally fellow survivors as Marcelo Perez did?
- Before and during the final expedition out of the Andes, Roberto Canessa expressed doubts about the wisdom of continuing. Both times Nando Parrado issued an ultimatum: "I'm going on whether you go back or not." *Would you* have done the same? *Could you* go on alone if your teammates abandoned you?
- Nando did not expect to succeed in his march to civilization, but he didn't share his pessimism with the others. Was this the right decision? Why or why not?
- As teammates on the Old Christians rugby team in Uruguay, the crash survivors had already grown to trust and depend on each other. How important was this camaraderie in the crisis? How can camaraderie be developed when people don't know or trust each other?
- When news of the survivors' decision to eat the bodies of their friends leaked out, many people were shocked and revolted. The Catholic Church in Uruguay and Chile absolved the group of any worries about it being a sin against God, however, and parents of the dead issued a statement in support of the survivors. What do you believe—is it a moral or pragmatic issue? *Would you* do the same in their position?
- Living so close to death made Nando more willing to take the risks necessary to survive. How can awareness of our mortality be an advantage?

Reporting In

Ask the Lord for an understanding of the power of love and how it can guide you as a leader or follower in your own life.

Hitting the Trail

(This is just for you)

In the crisis in the Andes, Nando Parrado finds his greatest strength in his love for his father. It propels him forward when everything around him seems to pull him back. What is it about love that gives us power like no other?

- "Only love," Nando says, "can turn life into a miracle and draw meaning from suffering and fear." What does this statement mean to you? Record examples here.

  _____

  _____

  _____

  _____

- Read 1 John 4:7–21, which includes the phrase "perfect love drives out fear" (v. 18). How does this illustrate Nando's experience in the Andes? How does it apply in your life?

  _____

  _____

  _____

  _____

- Nando questions why God allows some people to live many years while others have their lives cut short. It is one of the fundamental questions of faith. Some would say this is evidence that God is indifferent or that he does not exist at all. Some would say that God has given us free will, and because we sometimes make evil choices, tragedies are an inevitable result. Others, like Liliana, would say it is part of God's plan and beyond understanding. What do *you* say? Write down your reasoning.

_____

_____

_____

New Territory

(For those who want to explore further)

Read *Alive* by Piers Paul Read and *Miracle in the Andes* by Nando Parrado, the bestselling books about the plane crash and struggle to survive in the Andes.

- What were the qualities that enabled the survivors to endure for seventy-two days in the Andes? What were the turning points for the group?
- Which of the survivors did you relate to the most? Why?

Resources

Chapter 1: Death Zone

Breed, Allen G., and Binaj Gurubacharya. "Quest to Climb Everest Turned Deadly." *Bend Bulletin*, July 16–17, 2006.

Douglas, Ed. "Over the Top." *Outside*, September 2006.

Heil, Nick. *Dark Summit*. New York: Henry Holt and Company, 2008.

Stark, Peter. *Last Breath*. New York: Ballantine, 2001.

Chapter 2: With Gladness

Burnham, Gracia. *In the Presence of My Enemies*. Wheaton: Tyndale, 2003, 2004.

Grinberg, Emanuella, and Eliott C. McLaughlin. "Former Hostages Reflect on Return to Normalcy." CNN.com, http://www.cnn.com/2008/US/07/03/former.hostages/index.html.

Olsen, Ted. "Martin Burnham Went Out Serving with Gladness." *Christianity Today*, June 1, 2002. http://www.christianitytoday.com/ct/2002/juneweb-only/6-10-11.0.html.

———. "Martin Burnham: Willing to Go." *Christianity Today*, July 8, 2002. http://www.christianitytoday.com/ct/2002/july8/17.19.html.

Chapter 3: Dance with Death

Kramps, B. J. Interview by James Lund. August 26, 2009.

Pierce, Todd. Interview by James Lund. July 9, 2009.

Peter, Josh. *Fried Twinkies, Buckle Bunnies, and Bull Riders*. Emmaus, PA: Rodale, 2005.

Professional Bull Riders website, www.pbrnow.com.

Chapter 4: The Battle for Takur Ghar

MacPherson, Malcolm. *Roberts Ridge*. New York: Delacorte Press, 2005.

Milani, Lt. Col. Andrew. "Executive Summary of the Battle of Takur Ghar." US Department of Defense, May 24, 2002. http://www.defense.gov/news/May2002/d20020524takurghar.pdf.

Naylor, Sean. *Not a Good Day to Die*. New York: Berkeley Books, 2005.

Chapter 5: Cold Night in the Elk Mountains

Colorado Avalanche Information Center website, http://avalanche.state.co.us/pub/info_faq.php.

Chapter 6: Sailing for Glory

Deep Water (documentary). DVD. Santa Monica, CA: Genius Entertainment, 2007.

Jones, David. "Donald Crowhurst and His Sea of Lies." *Daily Mail*, November 4, 2006. http://www.dailymail.co.uk/news/article-414489/Donald-Crowhurst-sea-lies.html.

Knox-Johnston, Robin. *A World of My Own*. New York: W.W. Norton & Company, 1969.

Nichols, Peter. *A Voyage for Madmen*. New York: Perennial, 2001.

Chapter 7: The Open Road

Aller, Sarah. "Bike Tour of Colorado . . . A Family Affair." *Adaptive Adventures Experience*, Winter 2006–07. http://www.adaptive

adventures.org/aboutUs/Archives/newsletters/winter0607webL. pdf.

Author interviews with Drew and Jeanie Wills.

National Ski Areas Association website, http://www.nsaa.org/nsaa/ press/0506/facts-about-skiing-and-snowboarding.asp.

Wills, Drew and Jeanie. Interview by James Lund. July 2, 2009.

———. Interview by James Lund. July 17, 2009.

———. Interview by James Lund. August 28, 2009.

Chapter 8: To the Last Breath

Kurson, Robert. *Shadow Divers*. New York: Random House, 2004.

NOVA. Hitler's Lost Sub. DVD. Lone Wolf Pictures, 2000, 2004.

Singer, Michelle. "Divers Tell Tale of Mystery Sub." CBSNews. com, September 2, 2005. http://www.cbsnews.com/stories/ 2005/09/01/60II/main811960.shtml.

John Chatterton's website, www.johnchatterton.com.

Chapter 9: Fear and Friendship at the Top of the World

Alexander, Eric. Interview by James Lund. September 16, 2009.

Farther Than the Eye Can See. DVD. Serac Adventure Films and Outside Television, 2003.

Greenfeld, Karl Taro. "Blind to Failure." *TIME*, June 18, 2001. http:// www.time.com/time/magazine/article/0,9171,1000120,00.html.

Stoneman, Tonya. "Higher Summits." *In Touch*, June 2003.

Weihenmayer, Erik. "Tenacious E." *Outside*, December 2001.

Widdifield, Janna. "Journey to the Top of the World." *University of Denver Magazine*, Fall 2002, 17–21.

Eric Alexander's website, www.highersummits.com.

Chapter 10: Death and Birth in Blue John Canyon

Brick, Michael. "Climber Still Seeks Larger Meaning in His Epic Escape." *New York Times*, March 31, 2009. http:// www.nytimes.com/2009/03/31/sports/othersports/01ralston. html?_r=3&ref=sports.

"Being Aron Ralston," video, *New York Times*, http://www. nytimes.com/2009/03/31/sports/othersports/01ralston. html?_r=3&ref=sports.

Ralston, Aron. *Between a Rock and a Hard Place*. New York: Atria Books, 2004.

Survivor: The Aron Ralston Story (documentary). NBC News, 2006.

Chapter 11: Terror in Tanzania

Lamprecht, Leon. Interview by James Lund. June 9, 2009.

Neugebauer, Melissa. Interview by James Lund. March 11, 2009.

Tanzania Adventures website, www.tanzaniaquest.com.

Chapter 12: End of the Rope

Amazing Stories of Survival. From the editors of *People* magazine. New York: *People* Books, 2006.

Morley, Patrick. *The Man in the Mirror*. Grand Rapids: Zondervan, 1989, 1992, 1997.

Simpson, Joe. *Touching the Void*. New York: HarperCollins, 1988, 2004.

———. Interview by Andrew Denton. *Enough Rope with Andrew Denton*, ABC, June 9, 2003. http://www.abc.net.au/tv/enoughrope/transcripts/s879148.htm.

Touching the Void (documentary). DVD. Darlow Smithson Productions, 2003.

Yates, Simon. *The Flame of Adventure*. Seattle: Mountaineers Books, 2001.

Chapter 13: The Expedition

Lansing, Alfred. *Endurance*. Wheaton: Tyndale, 1999.

Morrell, Margot, and Stephanie Capparell. *Shackleton's Way*. New York: Viking, 2001.

NOVA. Shackleton's Voyage of Endurance. DVD. White Mountain Films/WGBH Educational Foundation, 2002.

Shackleton, Ernest. *South*. New York: Carroll & Graf Publishers, 1998.

Sullivan, Robert, and Robert Andreas. *The Greatest Adventures of All Time*. Des Moines: LIFE Books, 2000.

Chapter 14: Nightmare in Mogadishu

Bahe, Elizabeth. "Active Duty." *Worldwide Challenge*, January/ February 2003.

Bowden, Mark. *Black Hawk Down*. New York: Signet, 1999, 2000.

"On the Set" bonus featurette. *Black Hawk Down*. DVD. Columbia Pictures, 2001.

Struecker, Jeff. *The Road to Unafraid*. Nashville: W Publishing Group, 2006.

Chapter 15: Death Trap

Maclean, John N. *Fire on the Mountain*. New York: William Morrow & Company, 1999.

———. *Fire and Ashes*. New York: Henry Holt and Company, 2003.

Maclean, Norman. *Young Men and Fire*. Chicago: University of Chicago Press, 1992.

Matthews, Mark. *A Great Day to Fight Fire*. Norman, OK: University of Oklahoma Press, 2009.

Rothermel, Richard C. "Mann Gulch Fire: A Race That Couldn't Be Won." US Department of Agriculture, Forest Service, Intermountain Research Station, General Technical Report INT-299, May 1993.

Chapter 16: Love and Death in the Andes

Parrado, Nando. *Miracle in the Andes*. New York: Crown Publishers, 2006.

Read, Piers Paul. *Alive*. Philadelphia: J. B. Lippincott Company, 1974.

Nando Parrado's website, www.parrado.com.

About the Authors

Peb Jackson is the principal of Jackson Consulting Group, assisting clients with public policy, development, public affairs, strategic mission needs, media, mentoring, and private-sector initiatives in Africa. He is the coauthor of *A Dangerous Faith* and a former executive with Spartan Oil, Azusa Pacific University, Focus on the Family, Generous Giving, Young Life, and Rick Warren. Peb is a regular adventurer, leading trips around the world with many more tales yet to be told. He lives with his wife, Sharon, in Colorado.

James Lund is an award-winning freelance writer, editor, and author. He is the coauthor of *A Dangerous Faith* and the writer/collaborater on titles such as *Stronger* (with Jim Daly), *Going the Extra Smile* (with George Foreman), and *Bruchko and the Motilone Miracle* (with Bruce Olson).

A former newspaper reporter and editor and associate director of publications at Lewis & Clark College, Jim lives with his wife, Angela, and their three children in Central Oregon, where he enjoys occasional "adventuring" such as hiking and river rafting.

What do you think about the stories and themes in *Danger Calling*? Do you have a story to share about your call to risk and faith? We want to hear from you! Visit www.dangerous faith.net to send feedback and tell us about your adventure. You can also learn more about the authors and their work and read what others are saying about *Danger Calling*. We may even contact you about how your story can encourage others to risk for what really matters.

Share more true stories of adventure with your son or your youth group.

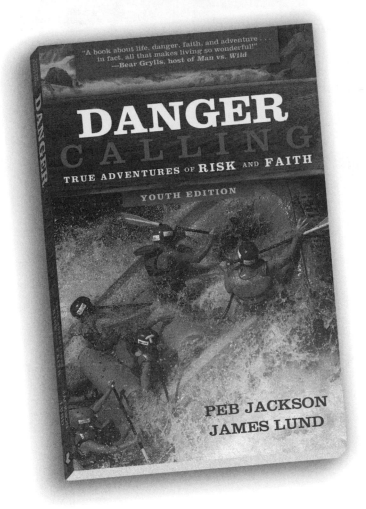

Includes eight brand-new stories not found in the adult edition.

STAND UP AND BE THE MAN
YOU WERE CREATED TO BE

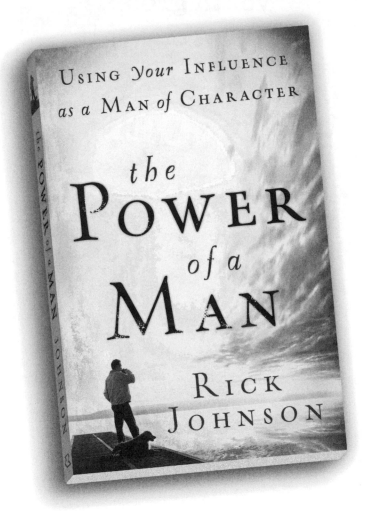

The Power of a Man shows men how to live
a life of great significance and healthy masculinity
in a world afraid of real men.

Family Expert
Rick Johnson
encourages and empowers fathers in their most important role.

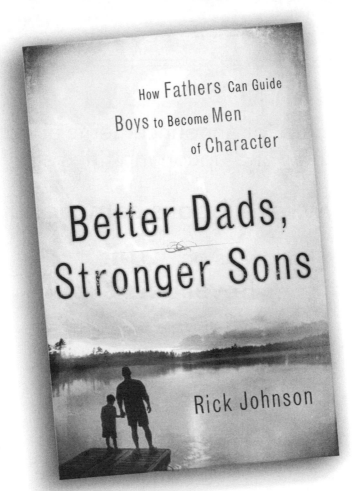

How Fathers Can Guide Boys to Become Men of Character

Better Dads, Stronger Sons

Rick Johnson